HERMANN GOERING

IN THE FIRST WORLD WAR

THE PERSONAL PHOTOGRAPH ALBUMS OF HERMANN GOERING

BLAINE TAYLOR

FONTHILL

Dedicated to Nicholas George Petite of Towson, MD, for his friendship, advice, humor, and help over the years.

Fonthill Media Language Policy

Fonthill Media publishes in the international English language market. One language edition is published worldwide. As there are minor differences in spelling and presentation, especially with regard to American English and British English, a policy is necessary to define which form of English to use. The Fonthill Policy is to use the form of English native to the author. Blaine Taylor was born and educated in Towson University, and now lives at Towson, MD therefore American English has been adopted in this publication.

Fonthill Media Limited
Fonthill Media LLC
www.fonthillmedia.com
office@fonthillmedia.com

This edition first published in the United Kingdom
and the United States of America 2014

ISBN 978-1-62545-046-3

Typeset in 10pt on 13pt Sabon
Printed and bound in England

Contents

Acknowledgments

To Stan Piet (photographic consultant) of Bel Air, MD, USA, who assisted the author in producing the Goering Album photographs shown herein from the Library of Congress, as well as from other sources.

To Mrs Erika Burke of Pearland, TX, who outdid herself in helping me translate some truly difficult German captions written by Goering himself!

And, finally, to the two local libraries that are always mainstays in my armory of helping hands: the Towson main branch of the Baltimore County Public Library, and also the Periodicals and Reference Rooms of Baltimore City's Enoch Pratt Free Library system, both in Maryland.

All illustrations are from the various collections held within the Library of Congress unless specifically credited at the end of the caption. The vast majority are also published here for the very first time anywhere. I particularly want to thank publisher Alan Sutton and his able staff for making this book a reality.

On previous page

Hermann Goering, cooling off in shallow water while off duty between his deadly, serial dogfights, is seen, wearing a still-popular 'muscle' T-shirt.

A Note Regarding the Photography

The majority of the images in this book come from the extensive collections held in the Library of Congress, predominantly the Hermann Goering Archive.

Goering was a keen photographer and true to character and happily for posterity he was vain, and liked having many photographs taken of himself.

Amateur photography was in its infancy in the first decades of the twentieth century and the equipment used was of poor standard and wartime photographic materials were also sub-standard. Furthermore, many of the photographs in Hermann Goering's personal albums were little more than contact prints, and therefore the images reproduced in this book are substantial enlargements from the originals.

During the 1960s when archival rules and regulations were less stringent the author was allowed to personally handle the Hermann Goering albums and was also allowed to photograph them. The photographs reproduced in this book are therefore mainly from the author's personal collection of copy prints.

Many of the images are of extremely poor quality, but have been reproduced because of their subject interest. The author and publisher apologize for the low quality of imagery, but assure the reader that every effort has been made to get the best result possible from poor, grainy and damaged originals.

A 'glamour shot' pose struck by a neat, trim Lt Hermann Goering in the early part of the Great War of 1914–18, in his unit's command map room. Worn on his tunic at right are the Iron Cross (top) and the German Imperial Flying Corps' Pilot/Observer Badge (bottom.)

Introduction

The author

As a young boy, I saw most—if not all—of the post-Second World War Hollywood 'sword and sandal' movie epics of the early 1950s. These included Greeks versus Macedonians, Romans against barbarians, and Israelites opposed to virtually everyone else, it seemed: Romans, Syrians, Egyptians, etc.

One of the battles that seemed to engage me—aside from that of the Alamo, and that still does—was the ambush of the British Redcoats and American colonials during the French and Indian War (also known as the Seven Years War) in the forest that resulted in the famous Braddock's Defeat. This was while I was living in the very pleasant red brick neighborhood of Govans, a suburb of Baltimore.

Next, we moved into Waverly, a gritty, tenement, working class locale more toward Baltimore's downtown center. It was here during 1957–1962 that I began reading about the early aviation combat fighter aces of the First World War, especially of the fabled Red Baron, Manfred von Richthofen, but also of his eventual successor of the famed 'Flying Circus' unit, Hermann Goering.

The first book that I read on the period was Floyd Gibbons' 1927 biography, *The Red Knight of Germany: The Story of Baron von Richthofen, Germany's Great War Bird*. The 1938 Errol Flynn-David Niven film *Dawn Patrol* became one of my favorites, and both this and my reading coincided with my building of scale plastic models of the German aces' aircraft that were then produced by two American firms, Revell and Aurora. I built several of them many times over!

I never dreamed then that one day I would be in a position to produce a series of illustrated books about these and other aces as I am today, having acquired copies of the as yet still largely unpublished forty-seven photograph albums of Hermann Goering in the American Library of Congress, and yet, here I am!

The publication of about 2,500 previously unpublished photographs from the personal and private albums of the late German Reich Marshal Hermann Goering, containing a reported 18,500 photos (or maybe 11,962 according to another source), has long been a cherished centerpiece of my desired intellectual contribution to our society, in a projected series of about six illustrated volumes overall.

The albums

Special Collections in the Library of Congress: A Selective Guide in 1980, states:

> Hermann Goering Collection. Biographical photographs of Hermann Goering, Prints and Photographs Division: The personal photo albums of Hermann Goering (1893–1946) were among the confiscated German materials transferred to the Library in 1947 ... and provide detailed coverage of Goering's activities during World War I.

A Library of Congress document entitled *Photo-Archiv Generalfeldmarschall Goering* adds: 'The collection documents in detail Goering's career from 1914–18 in two albums of 1,606 images.' An article published by Paul Vanderbilt of the Library of Congress, entitled 'Photographs of Nazi Origin' called the two albums 'an amazing collection formed by Goering as an aviator in the First World War, showing himself and his associates in the most minute detail ... The Goering photograph albums are said to have been found at Berchtesgaden in the Bavarian Alps, where Goering—like Hitler—had a retreat.' They may also have been found on his luxurious command train—codenamed Asia—instead, part of which was captured by the US Army in Bavaria in 1945.

Photographically speaking, Goering left a rich legacy of the history of that period—one, moreover, that was designed to show him in the best possible light to what he was certain would be a victorious Nazi posterity for the rest of the twentieth century at least. So sure was Goering that he would be rehabilitated in German history, even after the grim revelations of the Holocaust at Nuremberg, that he predicted to his Allied jailers, 'One day—perhaps 50 years from now—there will be statues of Hermann Goering all over Germany!' Indeed, they're now sold worldwide in many forms.

Housed in the American Library of Congress in Washington, DC, are the forty-seven finely bound volumes of his personal photograph albums, taken by a series of photographers, including Goering himself, especially in the first volumes covering the Great War of 1914–18. When I first perused them in 1967, one could hold the actual albums in one's own hands, but now—to better preserve them from both wear and tear, and even theft—they are available only through a microfiche viewer.

Enter Hermann Goering

The albums' coverage begins with Goering's life as a young man, and here we see him in an unaccustomed slimness that now seems surprising in one of history's most famous 'fat' men. His wartime career as a First World War airman unfolds in page after page of biplanes as well as scenes of the peaceful French countryside from the air—vistas taken by Goering himself in the role of aerial observer to help direct German Army ground-based artillery fire.

In the first set, we experience Goering's joy in his life first as observer and then as pilot, flights for which he was awarded many of his later famous medals: the Iron Cross 1st and 2nd Class, the most coveted *Pour le Mérite* (For Merit) 'Blue Max', founded in 1740 by Prussian King Frederick II—better known to history as 'the Great'. The albums end abruptly with the decline of German military fortunes in 1918, just as they do again—a world war later—in 1942.

Like most tyrants, Goering never saw himself as a despot. True, he gloried in the fact that Russian prisoners of war were eating each other in the German-occupied Soviet Union in 1942, and he also authorized SS Gen. Reinhard Heydrich—in the writing that later helped condemn him to death by hanging—to begin the systematic slaughter of six million Jews. His own self-image was hardly that, however.

Rather than being the executor of the Röhm Purge of the bully-boy SA Storm Troopers in 1934, Goering preferred to see himself as a cultured man of letters, a patron of the fine arts, a dedicated (and faithful) husband and father, an outdoorsman who loved to sail, ride horses, hunt, swim, and climb mountains—and all of that despite his considerable girth!

Indeed, Goering was all those things, which makes his life and career all the more difficult to understand in its totality, even now.

Of all the henchmen of the Nazi German dictator Adolf Hitler, Reich Marshal Hermann Goering was perhaps the most vain. Holder of a dozen top political and military posts within the Nazi hierarchy, Goering was creator of the second German air force, Reich Chief Master of the Hunt (and also in charge of all German forests), President of the German national parliament—then and now—the Reichstag; and Army General of Infantry among them.

Famously, Goering loved fancy uniforms and rows of gleaming medals—the more the better seemed to be his mantra—and yet, in all fairness to him, it must be stated that Goering wore no more than he was actually awarded. As one of his many biographers once wrote, a joke going around Berlin during the heyday of the Third Reich had the man called 'Hitler's Paladin' ordering a set of rubber medals so he could wear them in his bathtub! Another such yarn had him donning an admiral's uniform for the occasion, but that he did not have.

This is perhaps the most famous First World War photo of Goering, here displaying the Richthofen Squadron's famed blackthorn *Geschwaderstock* (unit walking stick) in his right hand, and—according to writer Hal Giblin—wearing the 1918 pattern parachute harness over his flight suit. This is the full frame of that famous shot, which also clearly reveals his Fokker D.VII's formal designation on the fuselage at left Fok. D.VII F5125/18. Note, too, the pair of mounted Spandau machine guns on the aircraft's cowling, above and behind Goering's head.

His vanity extended to owning many cars and motorboats (such as two big yachts named after his dead first wife), a palace in Berlin; the vast country estate also named for that same deceased spouse, Karinhall, outside the Reich capital, and two inherited castles, Mauterndorf and Veldenstein.

Because of these several baubles and toys, many in the West thought him to be somewhat of a buffoon, but he was far from that in reality. Rather, Goering was a cold, calculating, shrewd, and ruthless chief executive officer in Nazi Germany's corporate state. Indeed, Goering would feel right at home in today's modern American corporate climate as well, particularly among the financial barons of Wall Street. I can also easily see him hunting with Joseph Stalin, dining with Winston Churchill, and mixing cocktails with Franklin Roosevelt—all three men fated to be his deadly enemies during the Second World War.

Like his material wealth, the rest of Goering's life was equally out of proportion, truly larger than life itself, to a degree. As the number two man in Nazi Germany for most of twelve years, Goering ruled the country's economy, created the dreaded Gestapo secret state police that he later turned over to the even more sinister SS chief Heinrich Himmler; built what was, at one time, the world's greatest combat air force, established the concentration camp system in Europe, looted the enslaved continent's great art treasures for his own homes and galleries, initiated game laws that are still on the books in Germany, but—surprisingly—tried to keep Hitler from going to war in 1939.

Although not generally realized, Goering opposed Germany's entry into the war, fearing that it would lead to a global conflagration that would destroy all he held dear, and in this view he was, indeed, proven correct. Although Hitler called him a man of

The very same aircraft, also seen in 1918. Famed aviation author Peter Kilduff says of this photo, 'Goering had Fokker D.VII F5125/18 painted entirely in white to make himself distinctive to his comrades.' To that I would add, 'and to his foes'.

steel in a crisis, ironically, Goering lacked the moral fortitude to stand up to the Führer himself. Even though, during the First World War, Goering had been a celebrated and highly decorated airman—with the ear of the Imperial German Crown Prince—he deferred during the Nazi era to the lowly former L/Cpl Adolf Hitler, who had served as an unknown messenger in the trenches below him.

Goering ended that war as the last commander of the famed Richthofen Squadron who was also a famous air ace himself, and thus was of great value to the struggling politician Hitler in gaining access to Germany's former Imperial and Royal ruling houses, as well as its arch-conservative financiers, generals, and admirals in the pre-Third Reich era.

Indeed, while Goering was a salesman for BMW/Bavarian Motor Works aircraft engines in Berlin, he was also the Führer's financial 'bagman' with top German industrialist donors to the Nazis, helping finance Hitler's two presidential election campaigns in 1932. This was just before the Nazis achieved political office legally on 30 January 1933, when Hitler was appointed Reich Chancellor, and with him, Goering as Prussian Prime Minister in charge of the police, among other posts.

Goering founded the Luftwaffe in 1935, and became the highest ranking German military officer three years later as its field marshal. Had Hitler died or been removed from office in 1938—when Goering was only 45 years old—the latter might have succeeded his Führer, most likely keeping the country out of war, and retired as an elder statesman.

His second wife—German stage actress Emmy Sonnemann—died at the age of 81 in 1973, and their daughter, Edda Goering, (born 1938), reportedly lives quietly in South Africa today.

As things turned out, though, Goering—in both defeat and disgrace—was convicted as a war criminal, and also for crimes against humanity by the Allied International Military Tribunal (IMT) at Nuremberg, Germany, in 1946, three months before the current author was born.

Germany's former showman—called affectionately *Unser* (Our) Hermann by the cheering Nazi populace before the lost Second World War—eluded the hangman's noose by taking a hidden cyanide poison capsule. His sensational suicide occurred within a maximum security prison in a crime that was solved (maybe) only in 1985, almost four decades after the deed, by the late Texas author Ben E. Swearingen. Goering's death—only a few hours before he was due to mount the scaffold steps—stunned the world's media, and delighted the conquered German people, as one can well imagine.

Debuting the Goering Albums

This book, therefore, represents the very first venue in which a solid mass of these mainly previously unseen photos have been published at one time and in one place. There will be more, in succeeding volumes.

That series of mine begins now with this seminal work, covering the period of his life starting with his family, and concluding with the end of the Great War of 1914–18.

This is the fascinating story of the future Nazi Reich Marshal and Luftwaffe/Air Force commander Hermann Goering in his dogfights over the Western Front. Also seen are the many planes he flew and the colorful people he knew personally: Manfred and Lothar von Richthofen, Bruno Lörzer, Ernst Udet, Oswald Boelcke, Imperial German Crown Prince Wilhelm, and many others. How Goering's experiences in the Great War of 1914–18 colored his later development emerges clearly in these hundreds of photographs from his very own personal albums, shot mostly by Goering himself but also by others in his circle.

Hermann Goering was as good a military writer with the pen in after-action reports as he was an aerial and ground combat photographer of sites, events, aircraft, and the men who flew and maintained them.

The Iron Partnership

Previous authors and writers on this initial period of Goering's illustrious career have tended to concentrate on Goering alone, to the detriment of others of importance who were involved with him. Accordingly, herein I have expanded the biographical focus to include two other men who played pivotal roles not only during 1914–18 but also later in the rebuilding of the second German air force before 1939, and its usage in the renewed combat of 1939-45. Thus, the reader will find here the wartime exploits not only of Hermann Goering but also of his two able comrades-in-arms: first, Bruno Lörzer, and then Karl Bodenschatz.

This was, indeed, the 'iron partnership' that was forged during the fires of the Great War—and a mighty, engaging saga it was. In addition, that iron partnership was reborn in 1933, and flamed tempestuously across Europe and North Africa during the Second World War. Thus, it is worthy of our attention, as seen and described in this new and unique way.

Blaine Taylor
Berkshires at Town Center
Towson, MD / USA
1 August 2014

Centennial of the Great War 1914–18

1

Hermann Wilhelm Goering 1893–1946

'Hermann Goering, Amiable Psychopath' is the title of an article published in the April 1948 issue of *The Journal of Abnormal and Social Psychology* by Capt. Gustave M. Gilbert MD, prison psychologist during 1945–46 at the trial of the major accused German war criminals by the Allied IMT at Nuremberg, Germany:

> Hermann Goering's earliest childhood recollection was bashing his mother in the face with both fists when she came to embrace him after a prolonged absence, at the age of three ... He laughed most heartily in describing this and similar incidents to me in his cell in the Nuremberg jail ...
>
> The mother—a woman of ... humble origin [we gather from Goering's reluctant remarks] had returned to Germany ... [for] the family reunion ...
>
> Hermann became fascinated by military display: the uniforms and parades, the officers barking orders at their goose-stepping soldiers. He said that there was never a moment's doubt in his mind that he would become an officer in the Kaiser's army when he grew up.
>
> The reasons were obvious: the lowliest second lieutenant—he had learned from his father—took precedence over a Minister of State in the rules of protocol at the Kaiser's court—even on the grand march into the ballroom at State receptions. So at the age of five, he gleefully donned the hussar officer's uniform his father had given him for his birthday, and since that time, he said, he had never been without a uniform in his life [except for the brief period of civilian dress forced upon him by the vicious Treaty of Versailles] ...
>
> He cared little for learning, although he was of superior intelligence. Goering claimed that he was also influenced by his royal heritage, represented by the portraits of his noble ancestors hanging in the halls of his castle. But in telling this, he was probably still letting his youthful fantasies run away with him, because the noble war criminal—Baron (Konstantin) von Neurath—assured me that Goering had no noble ancestry, but was only an upstart brat whose chief talent was smashing windows.
>
> The very fact that Goering sought to impress me with an elaborately printed genealogical table taking the Goerings back to Frederick the Great, Charlemagne, and St Elizabeth of

Thuringen, is more significant as a revelation of Goering's aspiration level and fantasy life than of his actual background ...

He boasted, 'Hell, I haven't been afraid of death since I was 12 or 14 years old!' and was able to cite several instances to support this. On one occasion, he was riding along a road in the Austrian Alps, when an avalanche started. Goering says he just stopped to admire the awesome spectacle of crashing rocks and snow boulders while other people were dashing around in terror, trying to avoid being crushed.

One carriage was, in fact, buried under the snow a short distance in front of him. He found it all very exciting, but somehow the personal danger did not seem real to him.

On another occasion, he was rowing on a lake with some boys, when they began to drift uncontrollably toward a waterfall at the end of the lake. The other boys were panic-stricken, but Goering says he told them, 'Stop jabbering! If we go over, we die, and there's nothing we can do about it, so why get excited?'

Goering admitted that he just never believed that any harm could really befall him ... Whatever the reasons, the early signs of aggressive leadership qualities were unmistakable ... His mother ... recognizing all his unusual qualities, declared with some trepidation, 'Hermann will either be a great man or a great criminal!'

In actuality, she was right on both counts, as events turned out.

At the age of 16, Goering entered the officers' academy of Lichterfelde near Berlin, the West Point of the Prussian military caste. Somewhat estranged from his family by now, he made his emotional transference all the more to the military authoritarian hierarchy, with the Kaiser at the top ...

There was also much in the life of a cadet that satisfied the amiable prankster in him. He dared not show the slightest disrespect for the officer instructors at the academy, but the poor civilians who taught certain subjects were the constant butt of practical jokes and outlets for the rowdiness in the classroom.

Then there were the good old war games with real soldiers, swords, and guns, with no father to punish you for reckless daring in storming a stronghold. On the contrary, the Kaiser liked good officer material with plenty of daring ... Germany's defeat brought an abrupt end to his heyday of glory and libertinism. The flight of the Kaiser destroyed some of the heroic illusions he had built up about this figure of supreme authority.

Goering's family antecedents: a counter view

In his 1962 study *Hermann Göring and the Third Reich: A Biography Based on Family and Official Records*, Irish author Charles Bewley presents a generally pro-Goering look at his subject (whom he knew personally before the Second World War). He notes that *The Goering Family: Preliminary Study for a History of Our Clan* by P. Goering was published in Münich in 1911, as Hermann was about to become an officer:

> [The family] belonged to ... the upper middle class. In spite of all its striving for distinction, no member had ever received the ... von before his name, that would've raised him and his descendants to the ranks of the nobility ... The first of the family to attain

> even a modest eminence was a Michel Gering [original spelling of the name], who—in the early years of the 18th Century—became Royal Office Manager of King Friedrich I of Prussia ...
>
> Peter Goering, born in 1784 in Wesel, is described as the proprietor of a wool and cashmere factory in Düsseldorf, who later became owner of a brewery, and a member of the city council ....
>
> Peter Goering wore a darkish brown wig and was seldom ill—a proof of his moderate habits. In the evening at 7 PM, he went to his lodge in his old age to a simple wine house opposite his dwelling ... His favorite dish was white beans. It is possible that these caused the gallstones that brought about his death with great suffering. At the end, he asked to have sung to him his favorite hymn, 'See, here stand I, King of Glory!'
>
> Almost contemporary with Peter was Wilhelm Goering, the grandfather of Hermann, born in western Germany in 1791. Wilhelm started his career as a medical student in Duisburg, but was removed from the medical school by his mother: 'I do not wish my son to be a licensed slaughterer.' ... He turned to the study of law, and rose to the position of war counselor. His wife was Caroline de Neree, reputed to be a descendant in the direct line from a brother of St Philip Neri.
>
> Through his son, Hermann's father, the family rose to its greatest eminence [yet]. Heinrich/Henry Ernst Goering was born in 1838. After a university career in which he distinguished himself in the student dueling corps, he served in the 8th Jager Regiment in Wetzlar, and—after some years as an officer in the Reserve—took part in the wars of 1866 (Austria) and 1870 (France) in the 29th Infantry Regiment.

Goering biographers Butler and Young (1951) asserted that Heinrich Goering graduated from both Bonn and Heidelberg universities. (His son Hermann never finished his post-First World War studies at Münich University, however.)

Bewley continues:

> For the next 15 years, he held the position of judge in a number of provincial towns, and in 1881 [actually 1885] was appointed by Bismarck as Reich Commissar for [German] Southwest Africa [today Namibia] ... Dr Goering ... showed himself worthy of the confidence placed in him ... in the proximity of a battle between the tribe of the Hereros and a bandit chieftain named Hendrik Witbooi.
>
> At the cessation of hostilities ... a mighty feast was given ... while the flag of the German Reich fluttered merrily in the breeze, there was a magnificent display of fireworks, of which the natives were at first in no little terror.
>
> A Protectorate was [later] duly declared, and the German territory in Southwest Africa notably increased ... Goering was recalled and appointed Minister to Haiti ... until 1896, when he returned to Berlin and—after a short time—retired from public service [in 1898].

The two Mrs Heinrich Goerings

Before taking up his Southwestern African post, Dr Goering studied British colonial administration in London, and it was there in 1884—according to author Ludwig Paul in 1998—that he married Franziska (Fanny), in the very city that his son became infamous for bombing during the two aerial Blitzes of 1940–41 (planes) and 1944 (rockets). Revisionist English historian David Irving lists the London wedding date as May 1885.

Going to Africa later that same year, Dr Goering and his second wife Fanny—more than twenty years his junior—were nearly killed during a native uprising that saw their home burned as they fled for their lives. Also in Africa, Dr Goering met British Empire builders Cecil Rhodes and Houston Stewart Chamberlain.

Paul also asserts:

> In order to provide his Governor and family with a measure of comfort, Bismarck gave them a coach that he had used during the Franco-Prussian War of 1870-71. In this comfortable wagon, they traveled all over the new country. Franziska Goering accompanied her husband even into those regions where there was sporadic fighting between the military protection forces [i.e., German colonial troops] and settlers against the Hereros, the Hill Damaras, and the Namanguas.

Governor Dr Goering was polite and tactful to the tribal chiefs, and earned himself many honors. On its many trips, the Bismarck coach was accompanied by an escort of seven German colonial soldiers and 100 native Askari troops. Later on, pictures of this imposing retinue were to make a deep and lasting impression on the young Hermann Goering.

Paul continues:

> But another acquaintance the Goerings made was to prove fateful for them. This was the German-Jewish Dr Hermann Epenstein, who had been in Africa for some time, and had become rich through trading ... He fell in love with Franziska, and later took her on as his mistress. When Frau Goering gave birth to her second child Olga in Africa, he took care of her, and made himself indispensable to the Goerings ...

Dr Goering left German Southwest Africa after almost 'six years of service', asserts Paul.

> He left an established German colony that extended from Cape Fria in the north to the Orange River in the south ... To the present day, Goering Street in Windhoek still recalls Hermann Goering's father ...
>
> Dr Goering ... was sent to Haiti as Consul General. He retained the title of Minister Resident. Out of this, young Hermann Goering later construed the paternal *Ministerprasident* when he spoke about the services his father had performed for the Reich overseas.

Dr Goering's first wife, Ida, had died in 1879 after giving him five children in ten years of marriage. Bewley continues:

> By his second wife—Franziska Tiefenbrunn Goering—a native of Münich and a Catholic, he had five [more] children: three sons and two daughters, of whom Hermann Wilhelm ... was next to the youngest.

Butler and Young describe the second Mrs Goering—known affectionately as Fanny—as:

> Chosen from healthy stock ... a gay, temperamental girl from the Austrian Tyrol. Impulsive, deeply emotional, fond of music and acting [all traits later shown by her son Hermann], Franziska seemed ill matched with her pedantic, meticulous Prussian husband. Yet they were happy enough ...
>
> On his father's side ... young Hermann was descended from a line of officials and officers. His mother's origins were more modest. Peter Paul Tiefenbrunn—Hermann's maternal grandfather—was a Tyrolean peasant, a yeoman well liked and respected in the neighborhood of Reutte, where the Tiefenbrunn family is still solidly established.

Posting to Haiti, and Hermann Goering's conception

The Goerings returned home to Germany because Heinrich's health was suffering by 1890, the year also when the young Kaiser Wilhelm II fired his patron at the Foreign Office, Prince von Bismarck. However, Dr Goering received a new, second diplomatic posting as German Minister Resident and Consul General in Haiti, assigned to Port-au-Prince. He was soon joined there, however, by Fanny and the couple's three children: 4-year-old Karl Ernst; 1-year-old Olga; and Paula, who was 6 months old.

Here is Paul's take on this period:

> Toward the end of 1890, Dr Goering's wife followed him to the island with her three children—Paula was just six months old—where life was not without its dangers. The Goering's house was attacked, and they had to defend themselves against horse thieves. A good rider—with a reputation for courage and daring—Frau Goering took an active part in emergencies of this kind.

According to the future marshal's first major biographer, his close aide Dr Erich Gritzbach, in his 1937 work *Hermann Goering: The Man and His Work* (produced by the Nazi Party and edited by Goering himself):

> When her husband had to go on long journeys in the discharge of his duties, she had frequently to defend herself against the attacks and robberies organized by the blacks.
>
> On three occasions, she was alone in the house during earthquakes ... Two years later, Frau Goering was expecting the arrival of her fourth child, and was anxious that it should be born in Germany [so he would be a Reich subject, maybe].

> When she was expecting her fourth child [Hermann] she went back to Germany in order to give birth there. Dr Epenstein found her rooms in the spa town of Marienbad near Rosenheim, where, on January 12, 1893, her second son, Hermann, was born.

Paul further asserts that he was baptized as a Protestant, and that, 'The Prussian Hermann Goering grew up in Franconia that was part of the Kingdom of Bavaria, and it was in Franconia,' at Nuremberg in 1946, 'that his life was to end,' his last words spoken with a Franconian German accent.

Gritzbach continues:

> Ten weeks later, she returned to Haiti without him, and he was left in the care of his mother's closest friend, a Mrs Graf. His father retired in 1898, and died on December 6, 1913, with his son Hermann weeping in uniform beside his grave, having already entered the German Army.

While accurate, this 1937 account left out a very great deal, as we shall see.

Dr Hermann Ritter (Knight) von Epenstein: the Goerings' alleged Jewish godfather

Returning from Haiti in 1896, the family lived for a while in Berlin's Friedenau until Dr Goering's retirement from the Foreign Service. Of this, Paul adds:

> When Frau Goering and her family came back from Haiti in 1896, Dr Goering was old and sick. She became Dr Epenstein's mistress, and her husband tolerated the relationship ... The Goering family moved into an apartment in Fredenstrasse, in the wealthy, middle class district of Friedenau in Berlin. They didn't pay any rent because the apartment belonged to Dr Epenstein, who had also settled in Berlin and had substantial property there.
>
> In contrast to the retired Dr Goering—who had no fortune, and was keeping the family on a pension—Dr Epenstein could afford anything he desired. Franziska loved luxury, and after she had become Epenstein's mistress, he took care of the Goering family. The penchant for luxury—so evident in Hermann after he became successful—had been nurtured in the surroundings and circumstances of his youth when—though proud of his father—his idol had been the rich Dr Epenstein.

Gritzbach provides quite a different take on this period in 1937, however:

> Young Goering was taken from Furth [where he had lived with 'good, old Mother Graf'] to his parents' new home in Friedenau. Several officers as well as businessmen were frequent guests at the Goering home. It was a source of great glee to young Hermann when his father's wealth [*sic*] and his mother's hospitality brought the officers to the house.

> Even though he did not dare to put in an appearance at those festive gatherings himself—merely peeping through the keyhole of the door at the uniformed men was in itself a thrilling experience. Later on, his father's faithful servant, Johann, had to bring to Hermann—who was in bed—a few swords and caps belonging to the guests 'to play with for just an hour'.
>
> And when his elder brother Karl—who was a cadet at Lichterfelde—came to the house with some comrades of his corps and young Hermann was allowed to sit with them, his delight was unbounded … Potsdam—the town of soldiers—was to him a real paradise. There was no other place that attracted him so much, except Berlin on one occasion when there was a great military parade staged in the city … and when Christmas came, he had to have soldiers—lots of them. He had a typical German child's love for playing with soldiers.

Every Sunday, the family went to see the Potsdam parades.

> In 1898, his father was pensioned. That meant that the whole family had to leave Berlin. This was a terrible blow to young Hermann. He wept for days on end at the prospect of parting company with his beloved soldiers.

Unknown to him, Dr Goering and Fanny had accepted the invitation to reside in a small house in the grounds of Dr Epenstein's Veldenstein Castle outside Nuremberg. He was by then a close family friend.

According to Irving:

> Army physician Dr Hermann Epenstein [no 'von' then] 'property owner of Berlin', bought it [Veldenstein] for 20,000 Marks on November 29, 1897; over the next 40 years, until it was formally deeded to Field Marshal Hermann Goering on Christmas Eve, 1938, this philanthropic gentleman would pour 1½ million Marks into the renovation and reconstruction of its keep, roof timbers, its inner and outer fortifications. Veldenstein Castle was the romantic setting for Hermann's boyhood.
>
> You must come and see Veldenstein Castle [Irving quotes his sister, Olga]. Then you will understand him [Hermann] better.

Dr Gritzbach rejoins:

> The child could not realize that he would have a new and even more beautiful home in the castle of Veldenstein, to which the parents moved with their children. But when he drove up along the slope of the hill leading to the castle by his father's side—and when they passed first through the outer gate, and then through the inner one, which was even more magnificent, being equipped with battlements and embrasures, and finally reached the central courtyard, and saw the castle tower and the deep stream beneath, and the vine-clad walls of the castle—young Hermann's heart throbbed with glee.

Irving adds that Hermann was a robust child who suffered only tonsillitis and scarlet fever. As a young man, he developed arthritis, but this would vanish never to return after his 1923 groin injury (having been shot by the police during Hitler's aborted Beer

Hall Putsch). Irving further states that although confirmed as a Protestant in 1908, young Hermann nonetheless attended Catholic school at Ansbach at first.

According to Butler and Young:

> *Ritter* von Epenstein, extremely wealthy—a man well known for his generous gifts to charity—had met Dr Goering in Haiti, and had taken an immediate liking to him and his wife. He was a Jew, but that was a matter of less account in Wilhelmine Germany—where Jewish industrialists and financiers who had done much to develop the Reich stood ... high in the Imperial favor—than it later became in Hitler's Reich.
>
> Epenstein's father had been a Dr Eppelles, Court Physician to the Emperor Wilhelm I, a man already rich from his father's speculations in land and house property around Berlin. The physician had been dignified with the title of *Ritter* ... and his son now settled down in the Austrian castle of Mauterndorf to live the life of a wealthy country gentleman.

Author James Wyllie stated that von Epenstein acquired Mauterndorf in 1894.

Play-acting soldier Hermann

During the Boer War that started in 1899, young Hermann—like most Germans—sided with the Dutch Boers over the English. Bewley writes:

> At a tender age, he signs his name as, 'Hermann Goering, Boer General' in the guest book of a country restaurant in the neighbourhood of the family residence, Burg (Castle) Veldenstein near Neuhaus on the Pegnitz—the same signature that, 30 years later, he showed to British Ambassador Sir Nevile Henderson.

Impatient—like the young Hitler—with formal schooling at both Furth and Ansbach, 'He was in no sense a brilliant pupil ... His highest aspiration—even in his most youthful days—was to become an officer, and play a role in his country's history ...'

Once, he pretended to be sick at school, and took to his bed for four weeks, until vacation time arrived. Gritzbach notes:

> His bed was crammed with tin soldiers that he set marching and counter-marching, and advancing to the attack in the folds of his quilt. He had two large mirrors propped up in the middle of the bed. When his comrades asked him why he did this, he replied, impishly, 'In this way, I treble my army! You chaps will never be field marshals!'

This was a stratagem he imitated in 1936 with his aircraft to fool the Allies when Germany reoccupied the Rhineland, and again in the Second World War, to confuse Hitler during 1939–42.

When Hermann was 10 in 1903, Dr von Epenstein took him to see Castle Mauterndorf in Austria, a country Hermann would help occupy thirty-five years later, in 1938. Gritzbach continues:

> It was in Mauterndorf that playing at soldiering began to have for him a deeper meaning ... He listened intently to the accounts of the stormy days of the migration of nations when the old Roman castle was destroyed, and to the details of the rebuilding of the castle by the Emperor Heinrich II, who also built Veldenstein ...
>
> 'I shall be a soldier,' he told his parents one day. 'There is no other occupation that I would dream of following ... I am not going back to school anymore. I'm going to be a soldier now.'

Bewley resumes:

> Through the intervention of Hermann's godfather—*Ritter* Hermann von Epenstein—it became possible to send the boy successively to the Cadet Schools in Karlsruhe (Baden) and Lichterfelde (Berlin) as a member of the Royal Prussian Cadet Corps ...

Von Epenstein: Jewish or not?

Bewley continues:

> Writers such as Frischauer (1951) and Trevor-Roper (1947) have given further publicity to Epenstein's alleged Jewish origin ... asserting that he had, 'embraced the Christian (Catholic) faith a few years previously' to Dr Heinrich Goering's return from Haiti.
>
> ...In fact, Epenstein was neither Jewish by race nor by religion. The circumstance that in his youth he had served in the exclusive Danzig Death's Head Hussars is of itself conclusive proof of this. [My own reaction to this bald statement is, 'Well, maybe.']
>
> He came of a wealthy North German family, and—after his military service—practiced medicine in Berlin and Thuringia. Throughout his life, Dr Goering had been his closest friend, and on retiring from his practice, he purchased Burg Veldenstein, allowing the Goering family to use it as a residence.
>
> Later, he acquired for his own residence Burg Mauterndorf in Austria, assumed Austrian nationality, and obtained the title of *Ritter* from [the Habsburg] Kaiser Franz Josef.

Paul asserts that this ennoblement occurred in 1910. In their 1962 biography *Goering* Manvell and Fraenkel countered, 'Any doubt as to Epenstein's Jewish origin is dispelled by the inclusion of his name in the *Semi-Gotha*.' The controversy continues.

Von Epenstein's godson Hermann

Bewley rejoins:

> ... The elderly and childless doctor ... regarded his godson [Hermann] almost as an adopted son. The boy Hermann ... physically ... was the type that innumerable illustrators have chosen as their model for the hero of a boys' adventure book ... With the luminous

blue eyes that were always to remain his most striking characteristic, the regular, almost classic features, the pink and white complexion saved from effeminacy only by his look of robust health, the slender build that as yet showed no sign of the heaviness of later life, he seemed not far removed from the type of Nordic youth that has always been the German ideal ...

To his brothers and sisters, he was the natural leader: the children by his father's first wife were too old to play an important part in their lives. Paula—the nearest to him in age—was always his devoted slave. Olga—older and more independent in character—was no less devoted. The younger brother, Albert—though never influenced by and frequently hostile to Hermann's opinion—preserved throughout his life the admiration and affection of their early years.

Hermann ... thought of himself at all times as their natural protector. His sisters recall how, as a boy, when he had money to spare, his first thought was always to buy them some trifle, and how—at the distribution of Christmas presents—it was to him a point of honor to pass on to them half the gifts he had received.

... The picturesque background of Burgs Veldenstein and Mauterndorf was a powerful influence in Hermann's development. His favorite amusement was the 'knight's play' in which the medieval occupants of the castle defended it against a host of invaders, he himself being naturally the hero and leader of his brothers and sisters, and the boys from the neighboring village. He is described as impulsive, high spirited, physically courageous, easy to control so long as he considered himself fairly treated, but obstinate to the last degree in cases of real or imagined injustice ...

One of his sisters speaks of him as 'a fanatic for justice'. Possibly his love for animals was another aspect of the same passion for justice: he had the habit of bringing home with him any stray dog, lost cat, or wounded bird that he found in the forest or in the village.

He was, in fact, a romantic of a peculiarly German type, and—like all romantics—he perpetually played the part of the heroes of his youthful imagination ... to live up to the ideal that he had set up for himself. It was a quality of mind that lay at the root of his character, and was destined to abide with him throughout his life. If it made at times for theatrical gestures or attitudes, that theatricality was never a mask for insincerity: his poses were not of those that hide the real man, but of those that reveal his essential nature.

His record at Cadet School was satisfactory, if not exceptional. When his course was concluded, he left with the commendation of the Kaiser.

Of his cadet record, Gritzbach adds:

He attended the Military Academy in Karlsruhe, and took to his studies and his drill very earnestly ... You can see today [1937] a bronze tablet erected conjointly by the town of Karlsruhe and his former fellow students. When many years later, Goering—then a prime minister and a general—visited the academy for the unveiling of this tablet and sat in his old room once more, the few members of the staff who knew him in the old days greeted him with great warmth.

His conduct as a schoolboy had been rather wayward, but he was a model cadet—and as a cadet, he left an excellent impression on his tutors. In the Military Academy at

> Lichterfelde, Goering got the final touches of his military training. He received personal congratulations from the Kaiser on passing his final examinations.

As a graduation present in March 1911, his father gave him 1,000 Marks, and with it, young Hermann took his father's chauffeur, Sepp (Joe) Rausch, with him on the first of many pleasure trips he would make throughout his life to Italy.

Gritzbach recalls:

> He had a narrow escape from death during this journey ... on a canoe trip on Lake Garda with his friend, Sepp Rausch, they were overtaken by a thunderstorm that capsized their canoe. They were both rescued by another boat ... 'It was the first time I had to fight for my life ... I don't know of any more wonderful experience than that of pitting one's own strength against the forces of nature,' Hermann recalled.

Goering was then 18 years old.

Here is Paul's account of Goering's cadet life:

> When he was 12, his father sent him to the Cadet Academy at Karlsruhe. His sister Paula was attending [finishing] school there, as were the daughters of Frau Graf, who had taken him in as a baby. The Baden ... Grand Ducal Cadet Goering now wore a uniform. When he had turned 16, he was transferred to the Central Cadet Academy at Lichterfelde ... He enjoyed the life.
>
> The Lichterfelde Academy was strictly run, and standards were high; a cadet passing out with honors could be certain of a career as an Army officer. Hermann's record had been excellent, and his final examinations brought him the highest honors that a cadet could achieve. He received high praise from Kaiser Wilhelm II, who congratulated him in person. Young Lt Goering was the pride of his family.

Goering family life with and without von Epenstein

Not too surprisingly, von Epenstein is not even mentioned in the 1937 Gritzbach biography, and for good reason, too. First, because of his being possibly partly Jewish, and second, due to Goering's mother allegedly being his once live-in mistress.

Apparently, notes one source, the von Epenstein-Fanny affair began in Southwest Africa, and continued when they returned to Germany to reside permanently. A rich bachelor until his marriage, von Epenstein took all five Goering children (a son, Albert, followed Hermann's birth) as his godchildren, not just his namesake Hermann.

Von Epenstein was described thus by Manvell and Fraenkel in 1962:

> A domineering man, von Epenstein was punctilious in his demands, and insistent on receiving a proper degree of respect. He would lose his temper if his guests were so much as a minute late for meals. He was small, dark, and fat, obsessed by the sense of class, though his father had been no more than an Army surgeon in Berlin.

> He liked to pretend that he was the son of a court surgeon, and he acquired his title of *Ritter* von Epenstein by donations presented in the right quarters, [in the same way that Hermann's Nazi rival Ribbentrop bought *his* 'von' after the First World War]. Epenstein remained a bachelor, traveling a great deal and enjoying life.
>
> He practiced little as a doctor, though he attended Franziska in Africa when she bore her first child.

His two castles—Mauterndorf in Austria and Veldenstein in Germany, fifteen miles from Nuremberg—were spacious, so he offered the latter to the Goerings as a home once Dr Heinrich Goering retired.

> It was at Veldenstein that Franziska ... lived as von Epenstein's mistress. Her elderly and complacent husband had to accept this situation on humiliating terms. Von Epenstein kept the finest bedroom in the establishment for himself, while Franziska slept in a hardly less well-appointed room situated conveniently close by.
>
> Heinrich Goering was not admitted to this part of the home; he had to sleep on the ground floor [at Veldenstein]. When the family visited von Epenstein at Mauterndorf, Hermann's father was lodged in a house that stood apart from the castle. He was content—or pretended to be—with the dignity left him in the title of Minister Resident that had gone with his colonial governorship.
>
> ... In his old age, he found some remaining comfort in drinking and skittles, and he exercised little or no control over his second family of young children. Franziska was to remain Epenstein's mistress for some 15 years. It was, perhaps, ironic that the relationship should finally break down just before Heinrich Goering's death [in 1913] ...

It is not difficult to see the effect of this situation on Hermann Goering as a child:

> His father became a nonentity, living on the past memories of his past service to Germany; his godfather provided the symbol of power and of possessions to which he was instinctively drawn, though he must at a comparatively early age have begun to resent the situation in which von Epenstein had involved his mother.

It ended in 1913, and the family moved from Veldenstein to Münich.

Here is Paul's account of the end of the long affair:

> Had the relationship continued a while longer, it is quite possible that Epenstein would have become Hermann Goering's stepfather, because—after the death of her husband—Franziska would have been free to marry. As the stepson of a converted Jew, Hermann Goering would never have played a role in the Hitler movement, and his life would have taken a different course ... His father was dead and—although he was Hermann's godfather—Dr Epenstein had married and could no longer be drawn upon.
>
> The officers in his [new] regiment considered Goering to be coarse; he was not refined enough for their taste.

In his 1974 biography of Goering, *The Reich Marshal*, Leonard Mosley writes:

> Twenty-seven years old in 1893, Fanny Goering was a broad-shouldered, full-breasted blonde whose pretty peasant face (she came from Bavarian and Austrian farming stock) was transformed by one feature—the blazing beauty of her astonishingly vivid blue eyes. It was her eyes that had caught and held the man who was now her husband, when he had first met her eight years before [in 1885].

He has Dr von Epenstein delivering Fanny of her first child and son Karl in Africa, and also states that his 'von' title 'had been granted by Kaiser Wilhelm II a few years previously' not only to 1893 but also thus long before Paul's 1910 date. 'He had appeared in her hour of need and saved her life, and she would remain everlastingly grateful to him, determined one day to repay him. As indeed she did …'

Mosley continues:

> A few hours later [after Hermann's birth in 1893], a horse-drawn sleigh arrived at the door of the Marienbad Sanatorium and *Ritter* von Epenstein was announced. Fanny gestured to the bundle in the cot beside her bed and proudly announced, 'This is Hermann Goering.' She had determined to name the child after von Epenstein if it was a boy. In fact, he was christened Hermann Wilhelm Goering, the Wilhelm being for Emperor Wilhelm II. 'Look,' she added, 'he has blue eyes just like mine …'
>
> He [von Epenstein] would appoint himself godfather of Hermann Wilhelm Goering.

By the time Dr Goering returned to Berlin in 1896, aged 58, Mosley asserts:

> He became a drunk … and he was usually speechless or inarticulate by mid-evening … When did von Epenstein and Fanny Goering first become lovers? Most students of the Goering family history would time it at about a year to nine months before the birth of Hermann's youngest brother, Albert … [in March 1895].
>
> With the birth of Albert, von Epenstein announced that he was adopting all five of Fanny's family as his godchildren … As he became older, Albert looked uncannily like the family benefactor.

Their sister Olga Goering recalled later, '*Pate* (Godfather) had made Hermann his favorite godchild until then, but after Albert's birth, he was always fussing over him. Hermann became quite jealous of his younger brother,' and the two did not speak from 1923 to 1935 due to Hermann's Nazi politics, but still maintained contact from a distance via letters. Later on, Albert characterized his brother not as the 'Iron Man' but instead as 'very soft'.

'That young Hermann Goering was aware of his mother's liaison with his godfather seems certain,' Mosley asserts. 'We never had any doubt about it,' Professor Hans Thirring said later. Mosley explains:

> Prof. Thirring and his brother were also godchildren of *Ritter* von Epenstein, who was

one of their father's closest friends. It was Thirring Sr who had found Mauterndorf for his friend and completed the arrangements for its purchase [as his realtor, in effect].

'Everyone who stayed at Mauterndorf accepted the situation, and it did not seem to trouble Hermann or the other Goering children at all ... It was Hermann who actually fought and badly bloodied the nose of a boy visitor in the village who remarked that *Pate* had won his title from the Kaiser with money, rather than with brave deeds,' avowed Prof. Thirring.

Ritter von Epenstein was a Roman Catholic, and he made a great show each Sunday ... of leading his guests and his godchildren into the village church, but, in fact, his father was Jewish. A doctor at the court of King Frederick Wilhelm IV of Prussia [(older brother to the later Kaiser Wilhelm I], he had prospered under Royal patronage, made the acquaintance of the daughter of a rich Gentile merchant banker, and quietly converted to Roman Catholicism before marrying her.

But the family name went into the *Semi-Gotha* of the day beside all other titled German families of Jewish blood ... Hermann Goering found out the truth about his godfather's background when he was sent to a boarding school at Ansbach, in Franconia, in 1904. When he wrote an essay praising von Epenstein as 'The man I admire most in the world', the school authorities not only criticized it but also gave him a copy of the *Semi-Gotha* to read as proof that he was a Jew.

Ridiculed now by both faculty and students, Goering left school the next day and returned home. Mosley adds:

Gritzbach ... says Hermann left Ansbach because he was disciplined for leading a strike against the poor quality of the school food, and that he paid his way home by selling his violin to a fellow pupil. This version [Mosley's] comes from his favorite sister, Olga.

He also quotes mountaineer Goering as boasting:

I have no fear of heights. They stimulate me. Besides, any danger is worthwhile if—by risking it—you reach the top of the mountain. You know you will have a view few other men will ever see.

He emerged [at Karlsruhe] at the age of 16 with excellent marks in discipline, riding, history, English, French, and music. 'Goering has been an excellent pupil,' said his final report, 'and he has developed a quality that should take him far: he is not afraid to take a risk.'

From Lichterfelde, Hermann wrote to Olga, 'I am an inheritor of all the chivalry of German knighthood.' Mosley adds:

There were several much more mundane but no less enjoyable advantages to being a cadet at Lichterfelde: great beer drinking revels, racing at Ruhleben, swimming parties on the Wannsee [Lake], and girls ... His eyes [were a] vivid greenish-blue, and their effect on the opposite sex was startling.

Meanwhile, not only was von Epenstein keeping Hermann's mother as a live-in mistress, according to Mosley, but also seeing other married women. When Lt Goering returned home, he found the odd triangle of his parents with von Epenstein was finally breaking apart after so many years. The *Ritter*, aged 62, had fallen in love with an unmarried woman in her twenties who had remained a virgin until he married her.

The end came early in 1913 when von Epenstein formally ended his affair with Fanny in person, asserts Mosley, only to discover that Dr Heinrich Goering's honor had finally been insulted. Thus, he and his family could no longer stay under the *Ritter*'s roof, and moved to Münich by late spring. Mosley further claims, 'For Heinrich and Fanny Goering, it was the last time they would see together the handsome old castle [Veldenstein] in which they had spent 15 years of their life ...'

When his father died, Hermann got leave from his regiment to attend the funeral. Mosley concludes:

> He spent the day and the night before the funeral helping his mother to go through his father's papers. As he leafed through the faded photographs, the old diaries and letters—and as he listened to his mother reminiscing about the triumphs and disasters in Africa and Haiti—it was as if he realized for the first time the stature of his dead father during the years of his colonial triumphs.

Feelings of guilt and loss overcame him at the cemetery, as Lt Goering wept for the father he had never really known, since a full sixty-four years separated them in ages.

In their own notes about Hermann Goering's early life, Manvell and Fraenkel state:

> The principal sources were ... in addition to the past biographies of Goering which we have consulted [as have I], the personal recollections of Misses Erna and Fanny Graf of Münich, and of Prof. Hans Thirring, the eminent physicist, all of whom knew Goering intimately when they were children together.
>
> It is Prof. Thirring who vouches for the intimate relationship that existed between Frau Franziska Goering and von Epenstein.

Thus—and I feel obliged to point it out here in all fairness to Goering—the entire story of the alleged adulterous relationship exists on the testimony of but one man, Professor Thirring, who may or may not have liked Hermann as a child, or turned against him in 1945, after his fall. It is possible, and even plausible.

Lilli von Epenstein—and Goering's engagement to Marianne Mauser, 1913–18

Although we are getting a bit ahead of our saga chronologically here, I want to complete this aspect of Hermann Goering's familial, personal, private, and social life before we go on to his strictly military career during the Great War of 1914–18.

Shortly after his breakup with Fanny Goering, von Epenstein married Lilli, a woman forty years his junior, and they lived together at Castle Mauterndorf in Austria during the First World War. It was there that Mrs von Epenstein held gay parties during the war, and where by then Lt Hermann Goering allegedly met his first love, Marianne Mauser, the daughter of a local landowner, while he was recuperating from an aerial combat wound he had suffered sometime during the summer/fall of 1916.

Goering told Fraulein Mauser, 'I am not like the Englishmen! They start a party at two drinks under par, I at two over!' Before returning to his unit on the Western Front in France, Goering asked her father for permission to marry his daughter, Marianne. As Goering had little personal money himself, the father agreed to a secret engagement only.

Prior to returning to combat with his unit on 3 November 1916, Goering went to Castle Veldenstein with Lilli von Epenstein, where he was reportedly surprised to find his mother Fanny Goering once more in residence. He was even more surprised that Mrs Von Epenstein and her husband's former mistress—Goering's mother—had become friends since he had left to fight the war!

Later, Fanny told her daughter Olga that Mrs von Epenstein had taken Hermann's hand and said, 'One day, all this [Castle Veldenstein] will be yours again—and so will Mauterndorf,' as those, apparently, were her husband's wishes. Olga Goering herself recalls, 'Lilli von Epenstein was always in love with Hermann, but he never guessed it. He could not possibly think that anyone could prefer him to our legendary godfather.' The story does not end there, however.

In 1918, with the war lost and Goering's own military career at a dead stop in his eyes, Marianne Mauser's father wrote to him thus: 'What have you got now to offer my daughter?' Goering telegraphed back, 'Nothing,' and their secret engagement was broken. Two decades later—as field marshal and the highest ranking member of the Third Reich's military—Goering revisited Mauterndorf, where Marianne Mauser still lived.

Inheriting both Mauterndorf and Veldenstein, 1934-38

The *Ritter* died aged 83 in 1934, leaving behind his widow, Lilli. Goering invited her to tour his own vast, new country estate outside Berlin, named Karinhall after his first wife, who had died in 1931. Like his father, Hermann Goering married twice.

With Lilli in tow, the late Dr von Epenstein's godson mused, 'What a pity the old man could not have lived to see all this! How I would have loved to have shown him Karinhall!'

At Fanny's death in 1923, aged 64, after a sudden collapse, the von Epensteins did not attended her funeral in Münich's Waldfriedhof Cemetery, where she was buried next to her late husband, but they did send a wreath with their regrets.

In 1938, Lilli von Epenstein deeded Veldenstein to both Hermann and his second wife Emmy, whom he had married in 1935, with Mauterndorf in now Nazi Austria to follow after her own death, just as her husband had wanted in 1934. She visited America, returning to Austria in the summer of 1939. On the sudden outbreak of the

Second World War on 1 September 1939, Lilli had a fatal heart attack while listening to a radio news bulletin relating Germany's invasion of Poland.

When Hermann Goering took over Mauterndorf, he slept in the bed where once had lain his godfather and mother. According to Mosley:

> Now the son lay there, with his Gobelin tapestries on the wall opposite, and a Lucas Cranach nude hanging above the canopy of his bed.
>
> It was an experience to savor, and Goering must indeed have felt like a feudal lord of the Renaissance, or even imagined that he was the *Ritter* von Epenstein himself ... He'd had his revenge on the man who bedded his mother at his father's expense, and the love of the dead *Ritter*'s wife to boot.

Like Bewley, Mosley, too, knew the living Goering.

David Irving fills in some blanks, 1989

Irving has Goering attending the Catholic Private Boys' School at Furth in 1902, then being sent to Ansbach in 1905 for three years, or into 1908, with his arrival at Lichterfelde in 1910.

> He sailed easily through his finals in March 1911 ... He got on famously with the military instructors and scored 232 points [or so he later claimed], 100 more than was needed, and the highest in the history of the academy.
>
> The surviving record [1989] shows that he gained a 'quite good' in Latin, French, and English; a 'good' in map reading, a 'very good' in German history, maths, and physics, and an 'excellent' in geography. On May 13, 1911, his ... company commander at the academy signed this report to Hermann's proud papa: 'I beg to inform Your Excellency that your son Hermann recently passed the ensign examination with the grade *summa cum laude* [highest honors]. Baron Richard von Keiser.'

Irving—noted for both controversy and doggedly pursuing original source material—found a diary marked 'Hermann Goering, German-Austrian Alpine Club, Salzburg' (Austria) in the archives of the US Army Military History Institute at Carlisle, PA, where I have also done research onsite. In 1990, I had occasion to speak with Mr Irving on the telephone while he was touring the US promoting his many fine books, which I continue to read eagerly.

The diaries detailed Goering's vacation hiking expeditions during the summer of 1911 with friends, among them his future brother-in-law, Austrian lawyer Friedrich Riegele. Mountaineer Goering noted proudly:

> We had to step out onto a ledge barely a hand's breadth, with a sheer drop down into Laserzkar. The hut and lakes seemed tiny down there—boy, it was windy up there! Straddling the knife-edge ridge like a horse, I crossed between the two peaks.

Mountaineering was a hobby he shared with several of his future political and military associates, among them Nazi Deputy Führer Rudolf Hess, Field Marshal Erwin Rommel, and Col. Gen. Alfred Jodl, although there is no evidence that any of them ever hiked or climbed together.

Irving concludes, 'Sadly, his personal papers were looted from his private train' (codenamed Asia) at Berchtesgaden in May 1945, among them the two war diaries that he wrote in August 1914, a private diary kept intermittently between September 1916 and May 1918, and five flying logs recording all his flights from 1 November 1914 to 1 June 1918.

> One of these private diaries is known to be in private American hands, but the owner has refused to let anyone see it. However, in 1941, 'court historians' began working on his military biography, and filled four green files with selected World War I documents. These green files ... are now in US Army hands in Pennsylvania. They include Goering's complete personnel record since 1905; 44 selected air reconnaissance reports, and extracts from war diaries, and personal mission reports.
>
> The unrelenting evidence of these documents is sometimes difficult to reconcile with the flattering Goering biographies [as we shall see later on our saga].
>
> Dreamy, physically brave, and romantic, young Hermann Goering was inducted into the infantry as a subaltern in March 1912 ... and at Gross [Greater] Lichterfelde ... passed the officers' examinations in December 1913. He would write in his curriculum vitae/résumé that he spent his spare time watching the airplane acceptance flights at Habsheim Airfield. 'My interest in flying,' he pointed out, 'was always very pronounced.'

Goldensohn's 1946 Nuremberg Interviews with accused war criminal Goering

On 21 May 1946, Goering stated:

> As far as my childhood, I don't see what importance that has on my adult personality. Maybe it has. That's your profession, and I'm no expert on those matters, but I have been thinking about your repeatedly inquiring as to my boyhood days. I've come to the conclusion that there was no difference between myself as a boy and as a man—today even. I believe that the boy had all the markings that later on appeared in the man ...
>
> People who knew my parents and me often said that my mental abilities were from my father, but my temperament and energy came from my mother. One explanation of their differences in personality might be that my father was a northerner, and my mother a southerner.
>
> The north German is very quiet and constructive. The south German is more lively and artistic. All great statesmen were north Germans, whereas all the great artists came from the south.
>
> My father was Minister in Residence, which was a titled position in the Crown Council [*sic*]. He was formerly a governor of German colonies in Africa. Maybe I'm different from

my brothers and sisters because I'm the only child not born in the colonies. Father died when I was 20, and I was already away from home for many years. I was a young officer at the time.

His death was not unexpected, because he suffered from diabetes for a few years. He was 74 when he died. He was strict and stern, but beloved by his subordinates. He was constantly planning, and had a constructive mind. She [mother] died at 64, 10 years after my father's death. I was more attached to my father for some reason. Mother was very good to the children, but I think I was out of the home so much I lost contact with her.

Father never abided by his diet, and drank wine and ate what he pleased right up until the end. My mother was father's second wife. My father's first wife came from western Germany.

Noted interviewer Goldensohn writes:

His mother did not seem to be a subject he cared to dwell upon. He showed me a large monograph written by a professor at a university that contained page after page of genealogy of the Goering family tree. The ancestors included princes, queens, and other nobility as far back as the 12th Century …

'I have always been interested in family history. Chromosomes are funny things, aren't they? They may skip a generation, and you can find children who resemble the grandfather rather than either parent. Heredity is more important than environment. Blood will tell …

'But the environment plays a great part in the development of a man. It is significant where a man is brought up: in the city or in the country, near a lake, or on the shores of the ocean …

'It's not just that I am a hard man because of my long experience in the Army and in politics. It's true that I saw plenty in the First World War, and during the air raids, and at the front in this war, but I was always a person who felt the suffering of others. To paint me as an unfeeling ogre who laughs in court at the atrocities is stupid.'

On 27 May 1946, Goering added:

Nobody knows the real Goering! I am a man of many parts, but the autobiography, what does that tell you? Nothing, and those books put out by the Party press, they are less than useless … I had a very happy childhood. My father was a high diplomatic official, very renowned, a lively spirited man who loved hunting, fencing, and riding. He was mentally superior and a good conversationalist … He loved to live actively, and did so until the end. He did not have a grey hair in his head—he was as blond as a young man.

Concerning his mother, who died when he was 30, Goering stated:

She was very clever, sparkling, but—like all women, without any logic or reasoning power. I think that women are wonderful, but I haven't met one yet who didn't show more feeling than logic … Mother was all feeling, and no reasoning. I don't mean she was unreasonable—far from it—but not like my father, who was cool and logical.

My own energy and love of life I inherit from my mother, but my physical appearance and mental structure are from my father.

Goldensohn adds:

Goering had three half brothers and one half sister. He had also two full brothers and two full sisters. He had little or no contact with his siblings, he said, because, 'The difference in ages was so great, and besides, the children all lived outside the family when I was a child.' He seemed loath to pursue the story of his siblings now, or of his relationship to them ...

He continued listlessly to describe his family and siblings. His two half-brothers—whom he rarely saw—were 76 and 66 years of age and still living [while Goering himself was then 52]. One half brother died at 25 of unknown causes. His two full brothers were two years older [Karl] and two years younger [Albert] than himself. His older brother died during the First World War at the front.

His other brother, born in 1895, named Albert, was, 'Never a party member.' He was here in Nuremberg for a while, but is now interned at the camp in Hersbruck. 'He lived in Austria and was opposed to the Party until 1938. Then I had him appointed to become the foreign director of the Skoda [armaments] Works in Prague. That was before the occupation of Czechoslovakia [that occurred on 15 March 1939].

In reality, I had nothing to do with his appointment, merely recommended it. He remained in that position until the end of the war. His position was not affected by my station ... He took things too seriously. We never really got along well together. For 12 years, we never spoke to each other because of Albert's attitude to the Party. Neither of us was angry with the other. It was a separation due to the situation ...

You ask me about my own brother, and I can hardly tell you about him! It's strange, but true, of all human beings. It just occurred to me why we were estranged: he was always the antithesis of myself. He was not politically or militarily interested; I was. He was quiet, reclusive; I like crowds and company. He was melancholy and pessimistic, and I am an optimist; but he's not a bad fellow, Albert!

Kilduff solves more mysteries

Writing in 2010, noted international aviation author Peter Kilduff provided a great deal more on Goering's early life, and, in the process, solved even more mysteries and answered many remaining questions, for which I commend him.

He notes that Dr Goering was born on Halloween, 'In Emmerich, a small city on the north bank of the Rhine River, a few kilometers from the Dutch border.' In 1918, one of Goering's idols, the Kaiser, crossed that frontier to go into exile when the Great War was lost and he was overthrown. In 1940, Hermann Goering's bombers leveled the Dutch city of Rotterdam.

Kilduff adds that Michael Christian Gering (born in 1649 at Rugenwalde), 'changed the family name—which, as an adjective, means "small, petty"—to Goering'.

Hermann's father, he asserts, was the son of a judge, and 'earned his doctorate in jurisprudence,' or as a lawyer.

In between the wars of 1866 and 1870–71 (in which he was a *Landwehr* or Militia officer), Dr Goering married Ida Remy. Kilduff continues:

> [She was] the daughter of a prominent industrial family in Rasselstein bei Neuwied in his native Rhineland, and eight years younger than he. Their first child, Friedrich Wilhelm, was born on October 29, 1870 ... After the war, Heinrich Goering was appointed a district judge ... A second child, Ida, was born on September 13, 1872, but died 17 days later. Heinrich and his wife had three more children: Ernst Albert on October 5, 1873; Friederike Wilhelmine Klara on July 16, 1875, and Heinrich Karl on April 17, 1879.
>
> Unfortunately, six days after the birth of her youngest child, 31-year-old Ida Goering died of 'maternity fever', related to poor hygienic conditions where she delivered.

Thus, Dr Goering became a widower, like his son Hermann in 1931. Her final three births and her own death occurred in Devant-les-Ponts outside Metz in the new German province of Elsass-Lothringen, formerly (and now) the French district of Alsace-Lorraine, taken from France by Germany in 1871.

His second wife and Goering's mother Fanny was already pregnant when the couple married in London on 28 May 1885, and that may well be why they wed in a foreign land rather than in their own. The wedding occurred in the German Chapel Royal at St James' Church, but they were married a second time in a German Lutheran Church at home before Dr Goering set off for Africa, alone. In May 1886, Bismarck promoted Dr Goering as the German colony's first Reich's Commissioner in Southwest Africa.

Their first son together—Karl Ernst Goering—was born on 3 August 1887 in the Rosenheimer Marienbad, according to Kilduff's research, and Fanny remained with a local family until 26 March 1888. She and baby Karl then joined Dr Goering overseas.

Their second child—Goering's favored sister, Olga—was born in Waldfischbach, a German settlement, on 16 January 1889, a few months before Goering's future Führer, Adolf Hitler. She had been delivered by the Austrian-born Dr Hermann Epenstein, Kilduff attests, the 'physician assigned to the region'.

Fanny Goering returned to Germany to give birth to their third child, however, and this was Hermann's sister Paula. Fanny remained in the Second Reich afterwards, from 4 June 1889 until 2 October 1891, or twenty-eight months. Meanwhile, states Kilduff, Dr Goering was granted in 1890 a recuperative leave home in Germany before he was sent on to his Haitian posting, to which Fanny and all three children repaired as well.

Because of disease in the Caribbean region, she returned to Germany at the age of 33 to give birth to her fourth child and second son, Hermann. He was born also in the Rosenheimer Marienbad, delivered by a midwife, and weighed 12 pounds.

Having returned to Haiti, Fanny again sailed back to Germany for the final time in summer 1894, alone, and Dr Epenstein had her settled in the previously mentioned Berlin suburb of Friedenau, where he also lived. She gave birth to her fifth and last child and third son, Albert Gunter, on 9 March 1895, attended by Dr Epenstein.

Kilduff notes, 'Most likely, during the 1894–95 time span, Fanny Goering and Hermann Epenstein began what would become a long-term love affair, which raises questions about Albert Goering's paternity.' Kilduff further places Castle Mauterndorf 'among the Tauern Mountains ... about 125 kilometers southeast of Münich,' in Austria; and Castle Veldenstein 'in the Bavarian mountain village of Neuhaus an der Pegnitz, some 30 kilometers northeast of Nuremberg.'

Here, young Hermann would boast, 'I am papa's favorite!' as he bullied his sisters and the area's boys alike into obeying him. This led eventually to his being sent to boarding school at Furth, as we have seen, at age 7, with his pet dachshund, Waldmann (Goblin).

Hermann Goering's own Jewish heritage

According to Kilduff, Hermann never learned of his own Jewish heritage because it was kept secret from him. He quotes Professor Dr Hansmartin Decker-Hauff (1917–1992) as writing:

> Goering was the only prominent Nazi who was from a 'good' family; the paternal grandfather was a Prussian administrative district president ... Yet Goering's mother—and this pained Goering very much—was a Münich beer garden waitress of questionable descent ...
>
> Dungern omitted, certainly from ... publication ... [Goering's ancestral link to the Swiss] money-changer family Ebeler, also known as Grunzweig, which was converted from Judaism to Christianity in the 15th Century.

As for his godfather, Kilduff notes that his 'father had been elevated to the rank of *Ritter* (Knight) in the non-hereditary nobility'. He paid to send Dr Goering's three sons from Ida—and also Hermann from Fanny—for expensive cadet schooling. Hermann idolized his older brother Karl in his flashy uniform, but still one of his teachers asserted, 'Hermann is a good fellow, but a bit difficult. He is a born revolutionary.'

Aged 16, on 1 April 1909, Hermann 'matriculated to Gross Lichterfelde, south-west of Berlin in the Potsdam district ... lean, muscular ... and 5 feet 10 inches tall'. Like Paul earlier, Kilduff also claims that Dr Epenstein received his 'von' in 1910, not from the German Kaiser but from that of Austria-Hungary, Emperor Franz Josef I.

Hermann boasted, 'When I become an officer—and that I will definitely be—there must also be a war right way. I shall distinguish myself, and get even more medals than papa got!' In 1912, he was commissioned on 22 June, the date that Hitler invaded Russia over Goering's protests in 1941.

Kilduff states that Dr Goering died aged 75 in the family's small apartment at Tengstrasse 38 in Münich on 7 December 1913, later to become infamous as Pearl Harbor Day. The seventeen-year-long affair between Fanny and their doctor friend had already ended, the amorous physician having taken up with Lilli von Schandrowitz, thus bringing the family to Münich, where Hermann would find fame as a Nazi in

1923. His godfather did, however, leave him some money, and a note inviting him to visit Mauterndorf again.

On 20 January 1914, Kilduff has Prussian-registered citizen Goering ineligible to serve in the Royal Bavarian Army, but his time at the Karlsruhe Cadet School in 1904 qualified him to serve in the Baden Grand Ducal Army. He thus began his formal military career as a member of the 4th Baden Infantry Regiment Prince Wilhelm.

In like fashion—during the heyday of the Nazi Third Reich—Goering would have both a main thoroughfare in Berlin and a *panzer* (armored) division named after him, the latter fought by US Army General George S. Patton Jr on Sicily in 1943.

At first, however, his fellow regimental infantry officers did not seem to take to him. 'The newcomer is snappish,' they opined.

Above left: Hermann Goering's parents; his father, Dr Heinrich Ernst Goering (1838–1913) in bicorn hat worn fore and aft, and ornate Imperial German Foreign Office uniform (left) with his second wife, Franziska (Fanny) Tiefenbrunn Goering (1859–1923). Born on 31 October 1838, Heinrich Goering was both a former jurist and a later diplomat who served as Governor of German Southwest Africa under the regime of Iron Chancellor Prince Otto von Bismarck. Born in Emmerich in Prussia's Rhineland province, Heinrich was the son of Wilhelm Goering (1791–1874) and Caroline Maria de Neree (1815–1886.) She was the daughter of Everhard de Neree (1772–1820) and his wife Catherine Freiin von Locquenghien (1775–1861) who was descended from—among others—Gräfin (Countess) von Metternich, and the then *Freiherren/ Baronin* (Baroness) von Schönborn, according to one source. Dr Heinrich Goering retired from the German Consular Service in 1898, and died in Münich on 7 December 1913, aged 75. Thus, he did not live to witness any of his illustrious son's martial and political achievements, like my own.

Above right: Jewish or not? The question of the actual ancestry of Goering's godfather—Dr Hermann von Epenstein (1851–1934)—is still debated among historians. Note the ornate gloves, sporty cap, and Death's Head skull and crossbones symbol affixed to its front. Goering later emulated his patron's flashy clothes. As one of Goering's earlier biographers noted, '*Ritter* [Knight] Hermann von Epenstein—Hermann Goering's godfather—was an experienced hunter, a gourmet, a successful chaser of women, and a collector of castles. He was also a half-Jew, a fact that did not prevent him from having a considerable influence on his [later] Nazi godson.'

Below: The personal items in accused Reich Marshal Hermann Goering's Nuremberg Palace of Justice jail cell during 1945-46 included small oval pictures of his mother and father (right), as well as some books, writing paper, bridge playing cards, matches, and a pack of American-made Chesterfield cigarettes. Goering's mother Fanny noted, 'Came of a Bavarian peasant family. Among Goering's paternal ancestors were the Eberle/Eberlin in Switzerland and Germany; among them the German Counts Zeppelin, including aviation pioneer Ferdinand von Zeppelin.' *(US Army Signal Corps, Ray D'Addario, Holyoke, MA)*

Above left: Author James Wyllie describes this early Goering photograph, 'Hermann von Epenstein with his godchildren. Hermann Goering (far left) holds hands with [younger brother] Albert (center).' The boy second from left may be Hermann's older brother Karl Ernst, and the girl at far right is probably either his sister Olga or Paula. Von Epenstein wears a jaunty hunting cap that was also later affected by godson Hermann. Other claimed Goering ancestors were 'German nationalistic art historian Hermann Grimm ... and social thinker Jacob Burckhardt,' according to another source.

Above right: Castle Mauterndorf in what was then Habsburg Imperial Austria. Wyllie noted that it was 'the larger of Dr Hermann (von) Epenstein's two fortresses and dazzled young Goering with its old battlements, towers, passageways, and defences . . .Taken over as a ruin in the 1890s by Dr Hermann von Epenstein, it was restored over the following years, becoming a favored retreat for Hermann Goering. He arrived here from the Obersalzberg in May 1945. In 1966, the castle was purchased by the Austrian government, which has since restored and opened the building as a cultural center.'

Goering's own photo (15 May 1941) of Castle Veldenstein outside Nuremberg in then Nazi Germany. It also still stands today. Here, too, young Hermann pretended that he was its medieval lord and master. He inherited both castles from Dr von Epenstein's second wife Lillli during the Third Reich. Kilduff has noted, 'With its scenic view over the Pegnitz Valley, Burg Veldenstein was the centuries old Bavarian fortress where Hermann Goering lived as a young boy.'

Left: After scaling the castles' walls, young Hermann graduated to climbing nearby rugged Alpine peaks, a practice he continued in later life, when he had put on the weight that he became famous for, as seen here. Goering later claimed that he was named after Arminius/Armin/Hermann ('Man of the Army'), the early German leader whose tribes defeated the three Roman legions of Publius Quintilius Varus in the famous Battle of the Teutoburg Forest in AD 9 that precluded the Roman Empire from ever acquiring Germania as it had Gaul earlier. Some historians believe Hermann was more likely named after his mother's alleged adulterous lover, von Epenstein, however. The question remains unanswered.

Middle: Hermann Goering's first supreme warlord was not Adolf Hitler, but the man both of them served under in the Imperial German Army in the Great War of 1914–18, His Imperial Majesty Kaiser Wilhelm II (1859–1941), also King of Prussia, seen here in the mid-1890s with cigarette in right hand and with the hand of his shorter left arm resting on the sword pommel. He reigned during the period 1888–1918, and was Imperial Germany's third and last Kaiser. Like Hitler later, 'Kaiser Bill' made of his moustache a political symbol. His Majesty wears the *Pour le Mérite* (not yet called the 'Blue Max') at the throat.

Below: Military Cadet Hermann Goering aged fourteen in 1907. Already, he demonstrated the requisite flair in presenting what later American singer Madonna termed, 'striking a pose'. His pale blue eyes were his most remarkable facial features. Peter Kilduff asserts that he was then 'attending a military preparatory institution in Karlsruhe, capital of the Grand Duchy of Baden'.

Above left: The senior cadet academy at Gross Lichterfelde where young Goering was molded into a military man,' Kilduff has noted of this view. In 1933, it became the home post barracks outside Berlin of the *LSSAH* Adolf Hitler Bodyguard Regiment, later Division. It was also where—during the 1934 Nazi Blood Purge of the SA Storm Troopers—that then Prussian Prime Minister Hermann Goering sent his victims to be shot without trial. After the Second World War, Lichterfelde became a US Army post during its occupation of West Berlin.

Above right: Goering's younger brother by two years was Albert Günther Goering (9 March 1895–20 December 1966), who served as a German Army Signal Corps lieutenant during the First World War. He was thought to be the son of Dr von Epenstein and Goering's mother, thus making him Hermann's half-brother, and possibly also his Jewish blood relation. The von Epenstein–Fanny Goering affair is thought to have begun 'about a year before Hermann's birth' according to one source. Albert is believed to have been unfaithful to three of his four wives, unlike his brother Hermann, who was—so far as is known—a loyal and loving husband to both of his, having married the second time as a widower of four years' standing. Albert Goering ended his life living on a German government pension, and married his housekeeper so it would be transferred to her after his death, a week later.

German Army officer Hermann Goering surrounded by his family's female members in 1916. He has captioned this, *left to right:* 'Mama, Paula, me, and Olga in Bad Tolz'. During his later life, Goering strongly resembled his mother as he gained weight. His sisters doted on him all his life, and indeed were with him as Reich Marshal when he surrendered to the US Army on 7 May 1945. By then, they had both married Austrian lawyers, as Paula Elizabeth Rosa Goering Huber and Olga Therese Sophia Goering Riegele.

Goering skiing with his mother (second from left) and maybe his sisters, at Bad Tolz on leave in 1916, called the 'Turnip Winter' in Germany because the British naval blockade was effectively starving the German home front. Other alleged Goering ancestors include the owners of the German pharmaceutical company Merck, as well as major German Catholic writer and poet Gertrud von Le Fort.

The Goerings, mother and son, December 1916. He has captioned this, 'Convalescing in Münich'. His good looks are evident, enhanced by his uniform and high, polished riding boots. Mrs Goering had a home in Münich until her death aged 64 on 15 July 1923, when her son was already a high-ranking member of the embryonic Nazi Party.

Goering's January 1917 caption reads, 'Ascent to the Wendelstein Mountain Ilse and me'. She was either a friend or possibly something more. Notice the cane in his left hand, a necessity for him since the rheumatoid arthritis he contracted in his legs on the Western Front in 1914. He was celebrating his twenty-fourth birthday on the 12th.

2

Goering from Infantry Officer to Aerial Observer/Photographer 1914–15

Transition

Hermann Goering—renowned in the literature of the Second World War as German Reich Marshal and commander-in-chief of Adolf Hitler's dreaded Luftwaffe—began his career as an airman in the First World War.

Many students of this earlier period may well recall that he was a combat ace with twenty-two recorded aerial victories, and that he was also the third and last commanding officer of the famous Richthofen 'Flying Circus' of the slain Red Baron, Manfred von Richthofen. How many recall, however, that he started his aerial career not as a fighter pilot but, rather, as an observer/photographer, or that even this happened purely by chance, in part because of an attack of rheumatoid arthritis? Indeed, like his fellow Nazi and later accused war criminal Rudolf Hess, Goering made the decision to become a pilot from the safe confines of a hospital bed!

It is a strange story.

Leonard Mosley in his 1974 study *The Reich Marshal* states, 'Hermann Goering was 21 years old when World War I began, and few young men on either side were more eager to get into the battle.' As we learned earlier, he was inducted into the infantry as a subaltern in March 1912 and passed the officers' examinations in December 1913. David Irving, in his 1999 work *Göring*, adds, 'On January 20, 1914, he joined his regiment. "If war breaks out," Lt Goering assured his sisters, "you can be sure I'll do credit to our name."' He was as good as his word, too.

Asher Lee in his 1972 study *Goering: Air Leader* adds:

> The young lad gave plenty of promise of physical bravery. In his early youth, he turned, during his holidays, to the arduous risks of mountaineering, and became a skilled climber for one of such tender years.
>
> By the time he was 15, he had scaled the 12,000-foot peak of the Grossglockner ... There are stories told ... of his utter fearlessness and general disregard for danger, but they square with one's firm knowledge of the way he acted later as a man in time of war.

He entered the military academy cadet school at Karlsruhe in Baden at the age of twelve, and transferred to Lichterfelde outside Berlin at sixteen, was commissioned a second lieutenant at nineteen, and wept in uniform at twenty at his father's grave at Münich in 1913.

As the fateful year 1914 dawned, Goering reported for duty with his first regiment—the Prince Wilhelm No. 12 Infantry—at Mühlhausen in German-occupied Alsace-Lorraine on the frontier, taken from France in 1871. It was here that he joined forces with the man who was to influence the course of the rest of his life, as noted by Lee:

> The most important event ... for Hermann Goering was his meeting with Lt Bruno Lörzer, who was to introduce Goering to military aviation, and so reset the course of his entire life.
>
> Lörzer was then a fellow infantry officer at Mühlhausen. He struck up a friendship with Hermann Goering that helped to sweeten the dullish routine of German garrison life ...

Combat Infantry Platoon Leader in the 1914 Battle of the Frontiers

'Once I am an officer,' Goering had jokingly told his fellow cadets, 'there's got to be a war!' and now—in August 1914—that prediction came true.

In *The Rise and Fall of Hermann Goering* German writer Willi Frischauer states:

> Germany mobilized. Lt Goering had his war. It was not the kind of war of which he had dreamed in his cadet school, or in his billet in Mühlhausen. The order to march arrived, but his regiment did not march in the direction of France.
>
> The first trumpets Goering heard in the war sounded a retreat. Before he knew what had happened, the Prince Wilhelm Infantry Regiment had evacuated Mühlhausen, and had been withdrawn behind the Rhine. Lt Goering was put in charge of a platoon, but it was weeks before he was able to go into action.
>
> The front was stabilized with the French Army deep in German territory [during what came to be called later the Battle of the Frontiers]. The German High Command, contemplating a major attack across the Rhine, was anxious to have details about the disposition of the enemy troops.
>
> Goering's platoon was one of the small formations sent out to reconnoiter the French positions. An armored train took them across the Rhine. Goering disembarked and, with his men, edged forward toward his old garrison town, which was in French hands.
>
> On the way, they conveniently 'requisitioned' a few bicycles, and—thus mechanized—went on their way.
>
> In the suburbs of Mühlhausen, Lt Goering seemed to forget the task with which he had been entrusted. Right there—near enough to hear their voices—was a group of French officers, a senior officer, a general among them. Here was an opportunity to strike a blow at the 'Red Pants', as the German soldiers called the French.
>
> Gathering his men around him, Goering explained his plan. They would take the French by surprise, and snatch the general from their midst to take him back to the train in triumph.

> It sounded wonderful, but before Goering could give the signal for action, a nervous NCO fired his rifle. The startled French returned the fire, and the great plan collapsed in confusion. A hasty retreat only just saved Goering and his platoon. They reached their train in the nick of time.
>
> Many years later, Lt Goering's first exploit in the First World War was described as an act of heroism. His superior officers at the time were less enthusiastic. The move—far from yielding any results—had endangered the invaluable armored train, and the whole reconnaissance operation.

Roger Manvell and Heinrich Fraenkel in their book *Goering* provide one more bit of information on this raid that is missing from the earlier Frischauer account:

> He equipped his platoon with bicycles, and at dawn this seven-man patrol pedaled along the familiar road to what had once been their base.
>
> Their first encounters with the French outposts were a little too successful, and with courage bursting in their hearts, they rushed on through the suburbs until they had passed under the railway bridges, which were in fact held by the French, and cycled into the heart of the city, where the enemy was in full occupation.
>
> Once there, Goering was quick to commandeer a horse. He intended capturing the French General Paul Pau by charging suddenly into the midst of the men surrounding him, catching him up across his saddle, and then galloping back to the German lines …

Mosley adds this further detail:

> Determined to bring something tangible back with him, Goering ambushed another French outpost on the way home … and captured four French *poilus* (soldiers). For this feat, Lt Hermann Wilhelm Goering was mentioned in dispatches for the first time, and commended for his daring and initiative.

According to Irving, in 1989, 'He saw only leisurely action as a platoon commander in the Battles of Vosges, Seenheim, and Lorraine, and then as battalion adjutant in the fighting at Nancy-Epinal, and at Flirey …'

Frischauer adds:

> In the many frontier skirmishes which followed, Lt Goering—now an adjutant in the 2nd battalion—conformed more rigorously to regimental orders. Under the orders of Capt. Tschersich—an experienced regular soldier—he developed into a conscientious officer, courageous, but cautious.
>
> He was in the Battles of Mühlhausen [10 August 1914] Saarburg, and Baccarat, a reliable observer officer, sometimes moving forward to bring back information, or directing artillery fire from exposed positions hard on the fringe of enemy-held territory.
>
> His closest friend in these days was Lt Bruno Lörzer, a happy-go-lucky regular, a little older than Goering, just as anxious to earn his spurs in this war. Neither of them had any

doubt that it was only a matter of months before they would be in Paris with the enemy prostrate at their feet.

In fact, it was to be twenty-six years before they would stand in Paris as conquerors—in 1940, another world war away.

Ewan Butler and Gordon Young in their book *Marshal Without Glory* write:

> Reconnaissance ... became Goering's specialty. He made a habit of advancing under whatever cover he could find to a spot as close as possible to the enemy lines, and thence, from some point of vantage, he marked the French positions which he could observe on a map.
>
> These excursions often exposed him to greater danger from the fire of German artillery than from that of the enemy, but he was never touched by the missiles of either side.
>
> As the autumn of 1914 approached, Infantry Regiment No. 112 marched out of Alsace and into France proper, where the regiment fought its way through the Vosges Mountains, and was engaged in its first full-scale action at Baccarat, south of Nancy. The rigours of this first campaign—the damp, the cold, and the exposure—did for young Goering what the earnest efforts of the enemy had so far failed to achieve ...
>
> To Goering's intense humiliation, he was struck down by a sharp attack of rheumatism in the joints of both legs. Evacuated to Freiburg in the Black Forest, he lay fretting in hospital.

Lörzer's intervention

Fate now intervened in Goering's career in a dramatic way. Lee resumes his narrative:

> He chaffed at the dreary inactivity of the hospital ward. When he discovered that his friend Bruno Lörzer had been seconded to the local air training school in Freiburg, he sent him an urgent letter. Lörzer went to visit Goering, and regaled him with aviation short stories that fired Goering with enthusiasm and envy.
>
> He went to visit the Freiburg air training school, and immediately filled an application for transfer to it. On the day that Goering's application was turned down, Bruno Lörzer qualified as a pilot, and was posted to an operational unit of the German Air Force.
>
> At the Nuremberg Trial in 1946, Goering was to hold much discourse about the rights and duties of an officer. He emphasized the importance of discipline and obedience, and stressed how impossible war would be if officers were allowed to do as they pleased, to move according to their inclination, and to attack or retreat as they thought best.
>
> Early in 1915, he showed his disregard of military discipline once again. The German Army authorities had ruled that Goering was to stay in the infantry arm, but he followed Bruno Lörzer to the Darmstadt base of the young German Air Force, and got his friend to agree to use him as an observer.
>
> For a few indeterminate weeks, Hermann Goering was a kind of unofficial, unpaid air gunner/observer in 25 Field Air Detachment of the German 5th Army, under the command of Imperial German Crown Prince Wilhelm.

A military court had sentenced Goering to three weeks' confinement to barracks for leaving his infantry unit, but the punishment never caught up with him. He spent the spring of 1915 in the skies of the Western Front in the observer's seat of Bruno Lörzer's plane. The Lörzer-Goering team was a success. They carried out a succession of reconnaissance flights in which Goering both photographed and sketched enemy troop concentrations and gun positions.

In accordance with the custom of the day, Goering used a hand camera and leant dangerously out of the plane over the side to take his pictures. The armament of his plane consisted of one ordinary Mauser revolver.

Frischauer reports the following incident:

> The German Air Force was as yet short of planes, and it looked as if Goering and Lörzer would have to wait some time for transfer to the front. They soon found, however, a way to expedite matters. On the Darmstadt aerodrome, they discovered a brand new machine. A few hours later, they were airborne, and on their way to the west, Lörzer piloting, and Goering in the observer's seat.
>
> The machine that was carrying the two hopefuls had originally been intended for a certain Sgt Ziegler. They were lucky that Ziegler did not mind the trick that they had played on him; 20 years later, he received his reward. Goering appointed him commander of the National Socialist Flying Corps (NSFK)—the SA/Storm Troops of the air ...

Irving disputed this alleged incident, however:

> Authorized biographer Dr Erich Gritzbach wrote that—having been rejected for observer training—Goering nevertheless moved with Lörzer to Darmstadt, and started flying as his observer in defiance of all rules and regulations.
>
> In fact, he was routinely posted to 3rd Air Reserve Detachment at Darmstadt for observer training on October 14, 1914. The Gritzbach legend maintained that Goering 'stole a plane' to join Lörzer at 25th Field Air Detachment. The personnel file shows this (regular) posting beginning on October 28th, with Goering flying as Lörzer's observer at Verdun until the end of June 1915, but again it makes no mention of a stolen plane.
>
> The detachment's war diary shows that, by mid-February, Lörzer and Goering were flying an Albatross, B990; they had picked up photographic equipment at Trier (Germany), and Goering had taken a rapid radio and Morse signaling course.

Imperial patron Crown Prince Wilhelm

Frischauer notes:

> The objectives of these air expeditions were the fortifications of Verdun, against which the German armies were now massing. Taking back the photographic plates to headquarters at Stenay, 20 miles northeast from Rheims, the two young airmen were frequently called

into conference with senior officers to explain and elucidate details of their photographs, and to give eyewitness accounts of their observations.

Sometimes—from a quiet corner—the commander-in-chief—the Crown Prince, 'Little Willy' to the English, would listen to the animated reports of the young men, often amused at Lt Goering's strong and unorthodox language. One day in the spring of 1915, Goering and Lörzer were in conference at Stenay when the alarm sounded. A French air group had been observed flying in the direction of Stenay, obviously planning an attack on the headquarters of the Heir to the Throne of the Kaiser.

Rushing to their aircraft to take off, it flashed through their minds that the Crown Princess (Cecilie) had arrived at headquarters the previous day on a visit to her husband. Bombs were already dropping as they engaged the French in the air. In a short battle, the enemy was forced to turn tail. The house of the Crown Prince had narrowly escaped a direct hit, but many of the headquarters buildings had been severely damaged.

That evening, Goering and Lörzer were asked to report to their commander-in-chief. Personally, he decorated them with the Iron Cross First Class. He shook hands with Goering and engaged him in a long conversation. It was the beginning of a friendship that was to last many years and—while of doubtful value to the Crown Prince—became extremely useful to Hermann Goering.

From this day [3 June 1915, according to Irving], he received frequent invitations to join the dinner table of his Supreme Commander. In this elevated company, he met many members of the wealthy and influential German aristocracy, whom he was later to convince that the Nazi Party was by no means a collection of low-born riff-raff, but included many an 'officer and gentleman'—like himself ...

Of the 3 June incident, Irving adds:

It was Lörzer and Goering—now flying a 150-horsepower Albatros—who, although unarmed, managed to force one of the raiders down. 'The two officers were rewarded,' the war diary records, 'with an invitation to visit His Imperial Highness, the Crown Prince.

Their mission reports gave both men a first-class opportunity of mingling with the top brass. Hermann pasted into his album snapshots of the Prince of Hohenzollern (Wilhelm) with him on Vouziers Airfield, Gen. von Knobelsdorf with Lörzer and himself, and other visiting notables. Irving continues:

On the last two days of February [1915] the war diary mentioned that Lt Goering had taken the reconnaissance reports 'in person' to brigade or corps headquarters. After particularly valuable reconnaissance flights over the dangerous armored gun battery at Côte de Talon, the two intrepid aviators were summoned to the royal presence on March 25th, and personally decorated by the Crown Prince, who commanded the 5th Army.

'The Air Force Lts Gohring [*sic*] and Lörzer,' recalled the Prince in his 1923 memoirs, 'were among those who displayed conspicuous dash and zeal.'

Goering became a frequent visitor in the Royal mess. When he strolled in, all eyes went to this handsome, broad-shouldered young man with the penetrating blue eyes and square jaw. He was good at his job, as the excellent reconnaissance photographs testify—clear, dramatic pictures of the enemy airship hangar at Verdun, the spreading maze of enemy trenches, the enormous craters left by tunnel mines.

The 'Flying Trapezist'

In his biography of Goering, Mosley writes:

> As a camera-observer, Goering's job was a particularly tricky one, and soon earned him the nickname of the 'Flying Trapezist'. The plane in which he and Lörzer flew was a two-seater Albatros whose lower wing—unfortunately for the observer—came directly under the second seat, so that it was impossible to point a camera over the side, and take a shot at the ground.
>
> Goering would wait until the plane was approximately over the target, signal Lörzer to go in low, and then climb to his feet. Gripping the sides of the cockpit with his feet and lower limbs, he would hang out over the side, and would signal Lörzer to bank the plane and 'skid' it at an angle, so that he could get a direct shot. In this position—holding on practically by his toes—with the plane under fire from thousands of guns down below, he would calmly go on taking pictures, and changing plates for each shot, minutes at a time ...

Butler and Young attest:

> His comrades of those days recall Goering as a good, reliable observer, with a flair for aerial photography ... On one occasion, he succeeded in identifying—at the first attempt—a battery of French heavy artillery that was preparing to shell the German positions, and in directing German counter-battery fire from the air by visual signals with success so that the enemy guns never came into action ...
>
> Visual signals were all very well in their way, but the use of wireless telegraphy would save time, temper, and energy. Goering accordingly set himself to master the technique of wireless telegraphy, and was one of the first officers of any army to operate a wireless transmitter from an aircraft.
>
> By February 1915, he was a competent telegraphist, and he became extremely expert in observing and correcting the fire of German artillery by wireless signals. Here again, Goering's impetuous temper—and a tendency toward insubordination—which was becoming increasingly marked, got him into trouble more than once.
>
> To look down upon the target and see that—in spite of his best efforts—the German guns were still shooting wildly—was often more than his rather limited patience could stand.
>
> On one occasion, the German artillery was shelling the village of Beaumont, and shelling it with singular lack of effect. Goering tapped back corrections, but the gunners plugged steadily away, ignoring his signals. At last, he ordered the guns to cease fire, and as he flew back towards the German lines, delivered himself of a blistering signal 'in clear', inquiring, impolitely, why the battery persisted in wasting ammunition?

> This disrespectful message—transmitted in plain language for every enemy operator to hear—brought down a load of trouble upon the head of its sender, and the episode almost ended in a court-martial, but Goering—not for the first, or last, time—argued his way out of the difficulty, and, having done so, reached the conclusion that he had been an observer quite long enough.

Thus, his days as 'Franz' (the German slang name for observer) to Lörzer's 'Emil' (pilot) were over.

Like Lörzer, Goering decided to become a fighter pilot, went to flight school, graduated, scored twenty-two aerial victories, and won the coveted 'Blue Max' medal. He would end the First World War as the third and last commander of the Richthofen 'Flying Circus', as we shall shortly see.

Again, Kilduff has unearthed new material:

> Goering wrote that, after arriving at Mühlhausen, 'Very quickly I reported to the Flying Corps, and in July 1914, was notified that I was on a list to receive training as a pilot. Frequently, I took advantage of my free time to take part in (new aircraft) acceptance flights at Habsheim Airfield. My interest in aviation was already very prominent.'

This seems to run counter, therefore, to the previous tale of Lörzer as having introduced Goering to flying—or was it something that Goering later made up in order to give himself more credit for the decision? In addition, Lörzer's visit may have reinforced a desire that Goering had anyway. Kilduff notes that Lörzer had been transferred to the Habsheim flying school six weeks before the war started, that is, sometime in July 1914. Lörzer had also been born at Friedenau, Berlin, where, as we have seen, Goering lived as a boy. Might their paths have crossed there? It is certainly possible.

Kilduff dates Lörzer's transfer to Habsheim as 15 July 1914. He has Goering fighting in the Battle of the Frontiers for seven weeks, being awarded the Iron Cross 2nd Class on 15 September 1914 for his combat role as a line company commander in the Battle of Mühlhausen starting on 10 August 1914. Kilduff asserts that during the Battle of Baccarat on 23 September, Goering's regiment was under heavy French artillery fire as it tried to take over the Fleury–Bernécourt railway line, with Goering himself leading a rout of the opposing French infantry in his limited sector.

It was also there that the future aviator experienced severe arthritic rheumatism for the first time in both knees, following earlier, but lesser, bouts in his life. Evacuated from the Vosges Mountains to an Army field hospital at Thiaucourt, he was sent on to a larger medical facility at Metz-Montigny, and later by train on to the Freiburg im Breisgau Clinical Hospital in south-western Baden, where the now famous visit from Lörzer took place.

His infantry combat days were over, it seemed certain, and he perished the thought of being assigned to deskwork for the rest of the war. Early Goering biographer Martin Sommerfeldt states that Goering invited Lörzer to visit him thus:

> Lörzer's training was nearing an end. When he returned from one flight, an orderly handed him a note: 'Visit me here in the hospital. Greetings, Hermann.'

> Ten minutes later, Lörzer stood before Goering's bed. There he lay, with his knees wrapped in cotton wadding. 'That is no wound. During the fighting near Baccarat, I got a bad case of rheumatoid arthritis. It hurts all over ... In a week, I will be able to stand up. It is still uncertain how long it will take until I can get back to the regiment.'
>
> 'Do you know what you will do? You will come with me to the frontlines as my observer,' asserted Lörzer. 'There, you will not need legs, and we can have your knees wrapped in cotton bindings. Then you will be warm enough.'
>
> 'Fabulous!' Goering replied.

Thus the first part of the iron partnership had been born. Kilduff breaks new ground also in asserting that Goering's first flight in an aircraft had actually occurred in 1913, when prewar flier Ernst Canter landed near Gross Lichterfelde outside Berlin and took Goering up in his two-seat Rumpler Taube (Dove). This was the same year also that Lörzer had his first aerial ride with aviator Viktor Stöffler.

When Goering's eighteen-day hospital sojourn ended on 12 October 1914, he entrained the next day for Darmstadt to join soon-to-be-pilot Lörzer as his observer. Kilduff attests that it was his godfather Dr von Epenstein's influence that got Lt Goering a legitimate medical transfer from the infantry branch of service to the fledgling air arm, and this, too, makes sense.

His new role was no martial cakewalk, however, as he had to learn quickly aerial photography, ranging ground-based artillery units, and also dropping hand bombs from above on targets below. 'Damn! There is so much to learn!' the later even more temperamental Goering thundered.

On 27 May 1946, accused war criminal Hermann Goering summed up his First World War service for Nuremberg IMT interviewer Leon Goldensohn:

> He launched into a description of his career from the time of the outbreak of the First World War. He was lieutenant of infantry at the front and participated in the first few battles until October 1914. He then joined the Air Force. He was an aerial observer until June 1915, and then he became a pilot.
>
> At first he flew a large bomber, and in the fall of 1915, became a fighter plane pilot. He was severely wounded in 1916 during an aerial battle. In the summer of 1918, he became commander of four squadrons, which was the largest single aerial formation in the last war.
>
> He remarked that toward the end, the English had the biggest air force, but the Americans had only a few poor planes, which entered into action only toward the end of the war.
>
> He said that his injury kept him out of active service for only three months of the entire war in 1916. For two months, he was confined to a hospital bed, and another month he spent recuperating at a mountain resort.
>
> 'Ach,' sputtered Goering. 'I live in the present, not the past. All of this reminiscing is like so much dead fish.' Obviously, his recital of his past was so dispirited, it was unenjoyable to him.

'A storm sent by God'

That is how the start of the Great War in 1914 was described by Goering in the 1938 biography of him entitled *Göring: The Iron Man of Germany* by British author H. W. Blood-Ryan. Goering's overall commander during the Battle of Mühlhausen on 10 August 1914 was Gen. Josias von Heeringen, described by the author as 'one-time Inspector General of the Prussian Guards, and in 1908 Minister of War ... in command of the German 7th Army Corps investing the town.' Blood-Ryan continues:

> Massing his troops on the Kolmar-Breisach line, he prepared a counterattack [against the French 'Red Pants'] leading up to the temporary success ... that Göring underwent his 'most peculiar personal war experience' [namely his role in the bicycle blitz commando action that failed, as we saw previously].

Blood-Ryan describes Lt Goering's observer career thus:

> Duty with the reserve squadron embraced new thrills. Aerobatics ... occupied his time ... The finding of hidden targets, accuracy in the handling of bombs, the use of aerial cameras—all gave a zest to the new, dangerous, and strange service to which he had voluntarily appointed himself.
>
> One day the plane in which Göring sat as an observer appeared over Wiesbaden. Suddenly, he espied a familiar house among dense trees. It was his brother's. Signalling to Lörzer to go down, they swept over the place at low altitude, dived, zoomed, wagged their tail in greeting, and flew away home.
>
> Upon landing at Darmstadt, the friends learned that the guard at Wiesbaden—knowing that German planes should not be flying so low—had fired upon them, thinking them at first to be an enemy scout.
>
> Göring—the daredevil and irrepressible.
>
> ... They left on detachment to Section 25 of the German Field Air Service, based on Stenay ... His early days in the Air Service were spent [doing] reconnaissance behind the French lines, bombing, ground 'strafing' with pistols, and camera work on the chain of forts surrounding Verdun.
>
> During his early service, Göring carried out many orders of great strategic importance, but the incident which won him his first war decoration [*sic*] is outstanding. Reports had reached German headquarters that extensive earthworks were being thrown up to take heavy gun emplacements.
>
> Rumour had already called it the 'Power Turret', and it was Göring's task to find its exact position. On his first flight, he located the position and brought back very fine photographs, on which were based the plans for its destruction.
>
> The German artillery found range and opened fire; battery after battery of 'heavies' pounded away at the French position, while Lörzer and Göring circled about, a few miles behind the French lines, guiding the batteries' fire by means of the none-too-secret method of rockets.
>
> At the same time, Göring drew a plan of the positions of the falling shells in relation to the desired objective and—flying back over the fire control—he threw his report bag,

containing the sketch, so skilfully from a height of 2,000 feet that it landed literally in the fire control officer's lap.

For another hour or so, he directed the batteries' fire from vertical observation until the 'Power Turret' which—if completed by the French—would have proved an almost insuperable obstacle to any projected German advance, was finally and completely destroyed.

Reward followed immediately. The Crown Prince himself—as leader of the 5th Army Corps—invested both Lörzer and Göring with the Order of the Iron Cross (1st Class) [as we have seen]. What was more welcome, they were granted short leave.

Their next assignment upon resumption of duty was to photograph the chain of fortifications around Verdun:

> For over an hour—with short interruptions for recharging [reloading] his camera—he hung head downwards, in his hands the heavy apparatus, onto the plates of which he trapped the image of every objective noted in his instructions ...
>
> In the spring of 1915, aerial warfare began a new development. Faster machines—with greater climbing power—fitted with new and improved apparatus, took to the air. The Germans and the Allies introduced the early form of aeroplane wireless—the sending of messages by means of Morse [code].
>
> Göring quickly mastered this additional duty, and his self-assurance was again made very patent in his first wireless message ... The year 1915 passed fairly swiftly, and the days were beguiled with bombing expeditions, fights here and there, and routine reconnaissance ...

Blood-Ryan also credits Goering with the following innovation, probably with information supplied by Goering himself:

> By tinkering with makeshift pieces of metal, he succeeded in mounting—along the nacelle of his plane—a light machine gun, which, while possessing no fine engineering principles, was yet used by him with salutary effect during the late summer of 1915 in his flights in the Champagne area. He was thus the first German airman to use a machine gun in aerial warfare ...

The outmoded hand-held Mauser pistol was thus soon retired from air combat.

Blood-Ryan continues:

> The aeroplane had revolutionized warfare, and its effect had proved more far reaching than even the most earnest supporter had dared to hope. The new Aviatik ... became the most popular German machine of this period. With this revolutionary weapon under his control, the airman became invaluable—in fact, he dominated the battlefield, and here Göring was in his glory. He was the acknowledged master of aerial fire control, and it was the German 'heavies'—with Göring and his like as their eyes—which extended over a range of vision of a hundred miles, that saved the German line of communications at St Quentin and east of Cambrai.
>
> The combination of long-range howitzers and aerial control—with instrument and camera—became and remained the master spirit of the war. To Göring, therefore, war became

> an intellectual pursuit of absorbing interest. With his genius for work—so often commended in German Army orders—he was able to read the mind of the enemy commander from the position of his bivouacs, the size of his concentrations, and the direction of his long line of transport vehicles. Beneath his hawk-like eye, the fog of war became dissipated ...
>
> The introduction of this machine into general service spelled *finis* [the end] to the observation duties of Göring. He applied for leave to undergo a pilot's instruction course, and was very soon back at the Aviatik Flying School at Freiburg.

Writing after the Nazi Party had taken office in 1933, Goering asserted, 'I myself fought on the Western Front from the first day of the war to the last ... At last came the bitter end, the terrible defeat ... Germany had lost the war, and her freedom.'

According to Kilduff, Goering completed his observer training in October 1914, and was assigned to Field Flying Section 25, or FFA 25, on 28 October. Lörzer arrived at the same unit on 3 November. The plane that they jointly appropriated to fly from Darmstadt to Stenay—forty kilometers north of Verdun—to take up their duties, came from enlisted Cpl Günther Ziegler, superseded as he was by two lieutenants—officers.

Their first joint combat mission together—with Goering as Lörzer's observer—occurred on 5 November 1914, almost four years to the day when the Great War came to a dead stop with the Armistice.

Lörzer recalled:

> As the last and newest arriving pilot, I received the oldest machine, one that had been declined by the senior pilots. The peak altitude of this aeroplane was 1,800 meters. I received my baptism of fire with it in the first weeks over Verdun. The French artillery fired very well! Even though we were not shot down, the loud racket of the annoying shots still made a deep impression.
>
> Later—in his report—my observer [Goering] gave a vivid description of the event. The sector of the front on both sides of the Meuse [River] and east of Verdun was entrusted to us. I carried out flights with the most ponderous machine and in such bad weather, while the other aircrews hesitated, and so our reputation in the Section was established within a short time.

Their aircraft was an Aviatik B.II, serial number B36/14, and was powered by a Mercedes 120-hp engine, and unarmed. Goering sat in the aircraft's front seat with his map, and pilot Lörzer sat behind him. As with Cpl Adolf Hitler receiving his Iron Cross from a Jewish infantry officer, so, too, did both Lts Lörzer and Goering also receive their Observer's Badge from Jewish Capt. Ernst Blum, on 12 October and 15 November 1914 respectively.

Two days later, this Teutonic dynamic duo flew their maiden bombing mission over Verdun, and that afternoon Goering took his first series of aerial photos over Verdun's famous Fort Douaumont. They first met Crown Prince Wilhelm after a mission on 23 December 1914, as recalled by Lörzer:

> The Crown Prince ordered us to report to him in person, and he was generous in his praise ...
>
> It became a rule that after special ... achievements, we had to report to the Crown Prince. Thus, Goering's role as an observer led to his becoming chief spokesman [for

> FFA 25]. In addition to his position as an observer, he was born for the role of spokesman, favoring at that time dramatic forms in his manner of speech.
>
> Our Section Leader—who was often present during the reports—did not approve at all with this manner of Goering's strong, personally emphasized description of overcoming all difficulties ... The Crown Prince, however, found pleasure in the narratives of the 'wild child', as he once called Goering. He was also greatly amused by occasional impudent comments that Goering made about superiors of all ranks.
>
> In addition to the official reporting sessions, personal invitations came from the Crown Prince that often brought us to his table in the company of his closest associates. It is surely understandable that two unknown lieutenants—who stood without any old Army connections—were quite taken by such treatment by their Army Leader. Over the course of time, the Crown Prince became a sort of protector for us.
>
> Subsequently—when I became a fighter pilot and fought over other Army sectors—he continued to be kept informed. As a consequence ... there arose among members of FFA 25 ... a constantly increasing dislike of Goering, who they spurned primarily for his overly strong exaggeration during the formulation of reports, especially his oral statements ...
>
> The critics were not without validity, and, finally, when I attempted to exercise moderating influence on Goering, he defended himself most fervently against such a restriction. He reproached me for my 'damned objectivity' because of which it would never be possible to give a vivid description of an especially dangerous flight or overcoming difficulties.

On 23 January 1915, the pair received new photographic gear at Trier, Germany. Eleven days later, they also received their latest aircraft, Albatros B.I B990/14 with a 150-hp Benz engine, brand new from the factory, according to Kilduff.

Writing to a girlfriend back home, Goering asserted:

> I don't want to be an ordinary person! Struggle is and remains essential for my life, whether in nature or among people [a sentiment also shared by his later Führer, Cpl A. Hitler]. I want to tower over the human herd, not that I will follow them; rather, that everyone will follow me.

The armored gun turret photography previously mentioned took place between 24 February and 3 March 1915, according to Kilduff, over the Côte de Talon near Fort Douaumont.

Here is Martin Sommerfeldt's account:

> According to ground troop reports, extensive preparations were in progress to install a high-caliber cannon that the ... staff felt was a serious threat. Goering had to determine the exact situation of this so-called 'armored tower'. During the first flight, he succeeded in finding the site and making very good photographs of it. Then thorough preliminary discussions of ranging fire against the 'armored tower' were held.
>
> [On 3 March 1915] Lörzer and Goering circled ... behind the enemy lines. From directly above, Goering observed the batteries' bomb craters, and directed their fire with a complicated system of flare pistol shots. At the same time, he made an exact sketch of the location of the shell hits ...

> They glided back over the position of the firing batteries and from 600 meters' altitude [as opposed to Goering's 1938 version to Blood-Ryan of 2,000 meters] Goering dropped it in a report pouch so auspiciously that it fell right onto the batteries' observation post, [again, as opposed to in the 'lap' of the post commander!]
>
> In only an hour, he had directed the devastating fire, and the 'tower' was completely destroyed [Lörzer wrote in triumph]. The reward followed quickly ... The Crown Prince personally presented both comrades with the Iron Cross 1st Class ...

Actually, as Kilduff discovered from his research, the awards ceremony took place on 23 March 1915.

As Wilhelm wrote in his 1923 memoirs:

> With much anticipation, the General Staff officers maintained the closest verbal [phone] communication with all reconnaissance units, and the splendidly vigorous fliers of ... FFA 25—always ready to take off!—speedily earned my appreciation and deepest affection ... Through their special zeal and daring, the aviation Lts Gohring [*sic*] and Lörzer, among others, distinguished themselves.

Underscoring the honor even more, Kilduff notes that only four German wartime aviators were cited by name in Wilhelm's postwar memoirs, thus more bright feathers in the caps of both Lörzer and 'Gohring'.

On 22 April 1915, Goering took forty-five aerial photos over Verdun, and five days later, made forty-three more north of the city, focusing on the forts and the roads that supplied them as well. One week later—on 29 April—radiotelegraphy was installed in their aircraft. However, they could only transmit, not receive, messages, 'due to engine and wind noises', Kilduff attests.

In May 1915, Goering was also armed with a 9-mm Mauser pistol that was clip-fed with twenty-five rounds that fired only single shots. In the Stenay exploit of 3 June 1915 already recounted, Lörzer asserted that 'Goering fired off the whole clip of ammunition' at the marauding French bombers. He went on:

> We were invited to have tea with the Crown Princess [Cecilie]. In addition to the esteemed recognition that was expressed with it, we did not forget to devour as much as possible of the pastry and coffee offered. The Crown Princess continually asked questions, and Goering and I talked until the good stuff ran out.

Kilduff notes that Goering's action in forcing back the attackers—with a pistol—was cause for celebration. 'Even Goering's detractors—who considered him a loud-mouth bluffer—recognized that this time, the bluff paid off.'

On 4 June 1915, they bombed Beaumont, north of Fort Douaumont in the Albatros B.I. As Goering later wrote, 'When the Fokker single-seat fighters arrived at [the] frontline, I requested permission to become a pilot ... On July 1, 1915, I reported to the flying school in Freiburg.' Likewise, Lt Lörzer left also for fighter pilot training at Görries, in the Grand Duchy of Mecklenburg-Schwerin, that very same day.

Goering's caption is '21 cm mortar in position'. Note the German Army *pickelhauben* (spiked helmets) and wicker basket shell coverings.

'Battery in position' is Goering's 1915 caption. The German Army artillerymen wear cloth garrison caps.

Members of the German Army wounded behind the Western Front mingle with enemy wounded. Note the length of the bayonets on the guards' rifles! The enemy troops were captured French colonial soldiers.

Captured French colonial soldiers being marched into captivity on the Western Front, photographed by Goering himself.

This Great War photo shows mounted German Uhlan lancers guarding French peasants (center), suspected of being *Francs Tireurs*, 'the First World War equivalent of today's terrorists or guerilla fighters'.

Goering's caption is 'Russian PoWs working on the railroad at Vouziers', 1915.

A German infantryman in a foxhole on the Western Front, the beginning of the trench system of 1914 that ended the war of movement, and thus stalemated the fighting for the next four years.

Goering's 1915 caption reads, 'Pontoon bridge instead of the blown up French bridge', as German troops approached the camera lens at center.

German ground machine gun (possibly a Maxim *Maschinengewehr '08*) and crew on a wartime airfield in France.

Typical Army office in the field, complete with typist and typewriter at right, and desk with rubber stamps and telephone at left.

Smiling German Army enlisted men with bouquets of flowers on an unspecified occasion in the field.

'Brunelles blockhouse officers' is Goering's caption.

German wartime airfield anti-aircraft machine gun section, with gunner at left and range finder at right, with mounted binoculars at center.

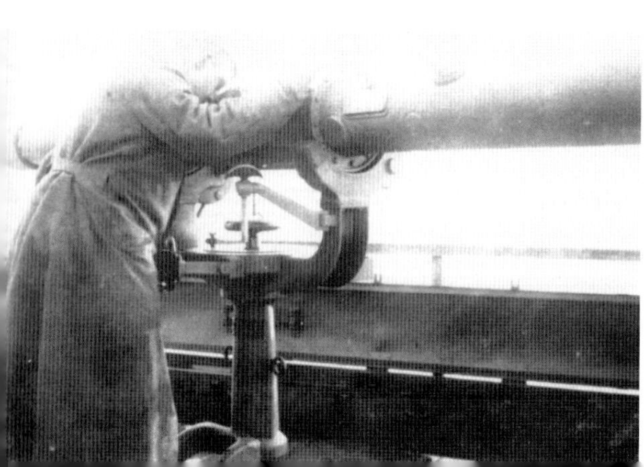

Goering's caption for this 1916 photo is '1Lt [Kurt] Schmickaly, leader of Flight School Metz', looking into a large range finder.

An excellent Goering action shot of a German railway gun firing, with the gun at left and the engine at right.

Above left: The first frame of a sequence of six Goering shots of a 'front visit' of Kaiser Wilhelm II, Crown Prince Wilhelm, and the latter's Chief of Staff, Gen. Schmidt von Knobelsdorf. Goering's caption for this frame is 'Crown Prince and von Knobelsdorf in discussion'. Wilhelm is at center wearing the busby cap, with his Chief of Staff at left center wearing the spiked helmet. The Kaiser is at right in right profile, also wearing a spiked helmet, and wading into the crowd of soldiers. The location is Stenay, France, the headquarters of the Crown Prince's 5th Army; October 1915.

Above right: 'The Kaiser gives the Service Order to officers and men' is Goering's caption for this October 1915 photo.

Right: 'The Kaiser, the Crown Prince, and His Excellency von Knobelsdorf' is Goering's caption, October 1915. Of the four men facing the camera in this frame, von Knobelsdorf is at the left, the Kaiser at center, and the Crown Prince is second from right, with the Death's Head skull and crossbones on the front of his fur cavalry busby cap.

'Kaiser Day in Stenay, distributing the Iron Cross after church' is Goering's caption for this October 1915 photo. The Crown Prince is again at the center in the busby cap. Goering's Imperial patron during the Great War, he also later aided him and Hitler in the Nazi takeover of Germany.

The Kaiser (fourth from left) is seen in right profile, distributing Iron Crosses at Stenay in October 1915, as the two officers at left render a military salute. Von Knobelsdorf faces the camera, third from left. Goering is the photographer, standing just a few feet away.

The Iron Cross awards ceremony at Stenay in October 1915 continues.

Above left: Goering's caption is 'The church of Varennes' (France), after bombardment, 1914.

Above right: 'Soldier's funeral', 1915.

'Burial of Lt [Werner] Noske of *Feldfleiger Abt. 25* Photo and Reconnaissance Section/ Squadron, who crashed in Swiry' is Goering's caption for this picture.

The last parade. Soldiers (left) act as pallbearers, with mourners following at right.

'Grave of a flier', 1914. Note the wreath and flowers in front of the Christian cross.

'Grave stone of Lt Wencher'.

"All Quiet on the Western Front", as reflected in the grave of a soldier who didn't come back. This was how ordinary enlisted soldiers were buried.

Above left: Crown Prince Rupprecht of Bavaria (left), German commander in Flanders, seen here with Gen. Sixt von Arnim (right.)

Above right: Commander of the Imperial German Army Flying Service since October 1916 was Lt-General of Cavalry Ernst Wilhelm von Hoeppner (1860–1922), seen here wearing the 'Blue Max' awarded to him on 8 April 1917, 'for outstanding staff service and achievements in organization' according to Edkins. 'He was one of two high-ranking, non-flying Air Service officers to receive the decoration amidst the many heroic aces who received it under a different set of rules,' like Lörzer and Goering. Von Hoeppner died on the island of Wollin on 25 September 1922, aged 62.

Field Marshal Gottlieb von Haeseler, 78, agreed with Crown Prince Wilhelm that the Great War was lost after the First Battle of the Marne in September 1914, and told the Kaiser, according to Holwig, 'The moment has come in which we must try to end the war.'

An officer—possibly Goering—saluting from horseback.

Gen. Sixt von Arnim (right, saluting) arriving for an inspection tour of the front. Note the command car with his pennant on the left fender at right.

Two German officers stand next to an aircraft at left on a wartime airfield.

A captured heavy British tank named *Hypatia*. Note also the picture album cornice in the upper left-hand corner.

Probably another captured enemy tank, with name obscured.

These are most likely German-made A7V storm tanks. Note the name *Hagen* on the left rear of the vehicle, and the iconic Iron Cross logo at center. The infantrymen at left wear the new 1916 German Army helmet.

A smiling Lt Hermann Goering (right) makes an appearance in cap and overcoat on a wartime German airfield. According to Manvell and Fraenkel, the aerial photographer in the spring of 1915 'was learning Morse in order to send down messages to base. His first message to a battery commander below is reported to have been, "You can stop firing. You won't hit the bloody target anyhow!" The observation was not even put into code ...'

Above left: Lt Goering, with walking stick, peers ahead into the camera's lens.

Above middle: Wearing flying goggles on his service cap, Lt Goering lounges in a chair outside with friends. Note the clowning prankster at right.

Above right: A seated Hermann Goering poses for a portrait that later became a Sanke postcard, wearing his Iron Cross and Observer's Badge below it. 'He was the best kind of young officer. His composed, regular features showed presence of mind and energy. His eyes were blue, tranquil, and arresting, and when his face and eyes became animated, one was aware of the unerring, sound common sense which lay behind them,' noted Karl Bodenschatz.

Above left: Goering's caption is 'Kasino [Club] in Gonnelieu on the Somme Front', October 1916. Kilduff has captioned it thus: 'Upon receipt of Baden's Knight's Cross of the Military Karl Friedrich Merit Order, Goering posed wearing it in an odd spot [center of his chest] and below Prussia's Hohenzollern Order. The rank order is understandable, but these awards were not worn along the button line of a tunic.' Goering also wears his Iron Cross (right top) and Observer's Badge below it.

Above right: On 9 May 1945, at Fischhorn Castle near Kitzbühel in Austria, 'The Eyes of Texas' look down on Reich Marshal Hermann Goering of the vanquished Second World War Luftwaffe as he poses before the flag of the Lone Star US (Army) 36th Infantry Division, the American unit to which he surrendered. At his throat he wears the Grand Cross of the Knight's Cross, and in a most curious fashion, his *Pour le Mérite*, or 'Blue Max', in his uniform coat lapel buttonhole, while on his right front are, from top to bottom, the Nazi Party Golden Pilot/Observer's Badge, the eagle signifying the awarding of the 1939 Iron Cross, and below them, his 1914 Iron Cross, earned during the First World War. Thus, Goering's cavalier wearing of his orders started in the Great War and continued after the Second! (*US Army Signal Corps, US National Archives, College Park, MD*)

Dog on horseback, a gag photo in the Goering Albums.

Lt Goering (right) on horseback with friends. The one at left also has a dog aboard.

During the First World War, Goering's mount jumps a fence.

A heavier Goering, again mounted, this time during his glory years during the pre-war Third Reich.

Goering wrote of this photo, 'Before the start on Sunday, an unlucky day.' He sits second from left, peering at the photographer, surrounded by fellow officers, and holding his walking stick in his left hand.

Goering (left) sitting with fellow officers on container drums.

Above left: From left to right : Goering (with cane), Lörzer, and an unknown officer, wearing overcoats.

Above right: Shirtless and wearing a hairnet, an off-duty Goering (seated, left) appears to be sunbathing as two men read behind him.

Future 'Blue Max' recipient and ace Otto Kissenberth with hand-held camera fitted to his Pfalz Parasol P39 aircraft, according to Van Wyngarden.

The observer of an Albatros C.III two-seater demonstrating the use of *Flieger Kammer* (Flight Camera) FK III in the oblique position. Manvell and Fraenkel in *Goering* state, 'The task of photographing from these primitive planes was extremely difficult and dangerous, and Goering had to lean right out of the cockpit, bracing his mountaineer's legs against the opposite side of his seat, for the under wing of the plane prevented a view to the ground below. He would stretch out from the plane, holding the heavy camera and exposing plate after plate with the lens pointed downward.'

A be-goggled and helmeted German aerial observer with a Parabellum ('For War') LMG 14 machine gun that he also operated. Note, too, the packed flares, grenades, and rockets aboard.

Above left: Kilduff notes, 'Goering struck a determined pose for this view of him at the controls of the AEG G.II 49/15' fighter aircraft. Goering's own caption states, 'Me in my *Jagd* [hunting machine] Albatros D3 2049', also a fighter. Note the black leather crash helmet and goggles in place.

Above right: Observer Goering (third from left) turns around in his aircraft cockpit at center. Note also the man at right taking a picture of Goering turning. Manvell and Fraenkel write, 'Reconnaissance was their principal duty. Goering—photographing and sketching the enemy positions and gun emplacements—was in his element. His skill and accuracy became famous. Based now on Stenay, in north-eastern France, he photographed the chain of forts surrounding Verdun.'

The photo of Goering turning in his seat that the man at right in the above (top right) photo took. Goering himself captioned this photo, 'Me with two observers'.

Pilot Goering (right) captioned this photo 'During flight', 1916, wearing two pairs of goggles over his black, leather crash helmet.

Goering's caption for this June 1916 photo reads, 'My observer, Graf von Schaesberg'. Note the machine gun mounted on the plane above. Goering as a pilot flew two-seat observation planes before single-seat fighters.

Below left and right: 'At our Kasino [Club] with our [dog] Hindenburg' is Goering's caption for these 1916 photos. Note the black leather crash helmet and goggles.

Nazi NSKK (Motor Corps) troopers in 1934, wearing black leather crash helmets. Minus the Nazi eagle and swastika emblem on the front, they are exactly the same as that worn by Observer/Pilot Lt Goering during 1914–16! Angolia and Littlejohn in 1994 state, '[Crash] helmets were made of either black leather or black Vulcan fiber (the leather protective head portion was 2.5 mm thick, while the Vulcan fiber was only 1.5 mm thick, but with greater strength). It took the form of a hard helmet with front visor ...' (*Innes, Heinrich Hoffmann Albums [HHA], US National Archives, College Park, MD*)

A German Halberstadt CL.II aircraft, photographed by Hermann Goering.

Overturned German Aviatik B.II reconnaissance aircraft.

Goering's caption is 'Stopover in Jametz', German GKFZ G.54 aircraft with right motor burned, 30 April 1916.

A German Rumpler C.I aircraft. Kilduff has captioned this photo thus: 'FFA 25 comrades 1st Lt Hellmuth Volkmann (standing by propeller) and Lt Hugo Weingarth (in the airplane) and their ground crew posed while Goering took this photo with his camera.' Hundreds of this type aircraft were built before production ceased in June 1917. A two-seat recon. and all-purpose aircraft, the Rumpler C.I had as its power plant a single 160-hp Mercedes D.III inline piston engine, and a pair of 7.92-mm machine guns, one being fixed and the other trainable, plus up to 220 pounds of bombs. Having a top speed of 95 mph, the Rumpler C.I had a maximum ceiling of 16,405 feet, a total takeoff weight of 2,866 pounds, and a wingspan of 39 feet 10¼ inches, a length of 27 feet 9 inches, and a height of 10 feet.

Goering's caption is 'My GKFZ Heavy Fighter Plane G49 in Schilzendorf', 1915.

Goering's personal caption is 'After the installation of the Metz airfield, before the take-off, my GKFZ AEG 49', summer 1915.

'My G49 [fighter] starting off,' Goering wrote of this photo, 1915.

Right: 'My second landing at Jametz in my [AEG] G49,' notes Goering of this 1916 photo.

Below left and right: The tail of Goering's AEG G49/15 fighter airplane.

Full side view of Goering's AEG G49/15 fighter aircraft outside a hangar, 1916.

'Over the clouds in my GKFZ', 1916.

Above and below: German AEGs.

German officers pose in front of an AEG G.II.

Above and below: A pair of side views taken by lens man Hermann Goering of his AEG G.II. Note the cowling-mounted machine gun at left and the engine at right.

A smiling Hermann Goering posing in front of his AEG G.II.

Suited up and helmeted for action, Goering turns around in the cockpit of his AEG G.II. Note the detail of the propeller and engine at right.

Kilduff has captioned this aerial shot, 'Goering's AEG G.II 49/15 was photographed in the air by another FFA 25 airplane on March 31, 1916.'

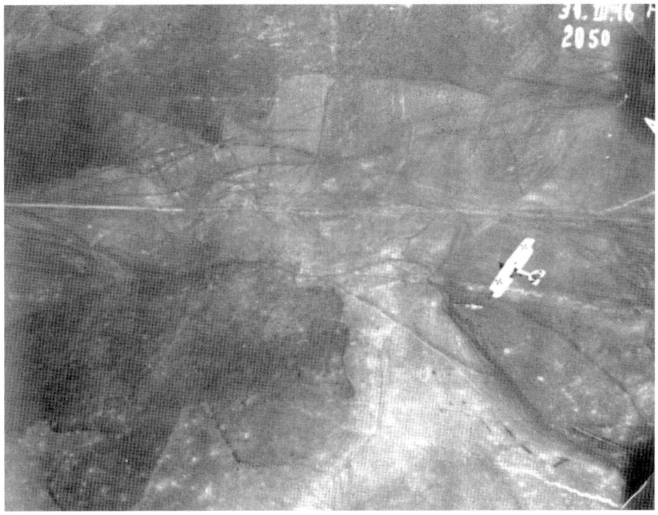

Another view of Goering's AEG G.II 49/15 fighter aloft, 31 March 1916.

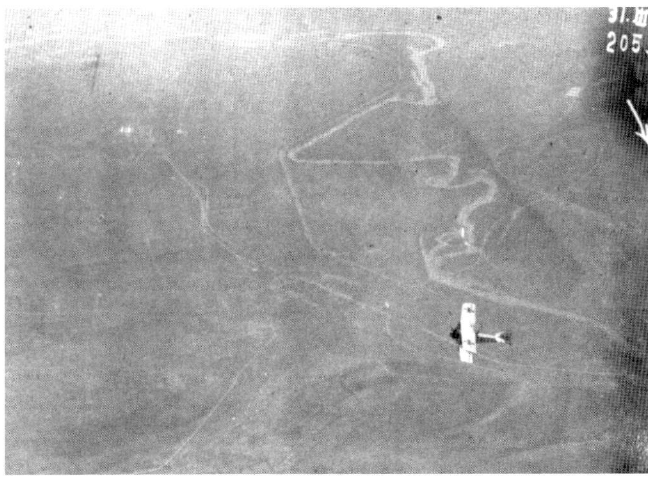

Another shot in the same series taken from above Goering's aircraft on 31 March 1916. Goering's caption for this scene is 'My GKFZ G49 at 2,500 feet over the enemy position north of Verdun.'

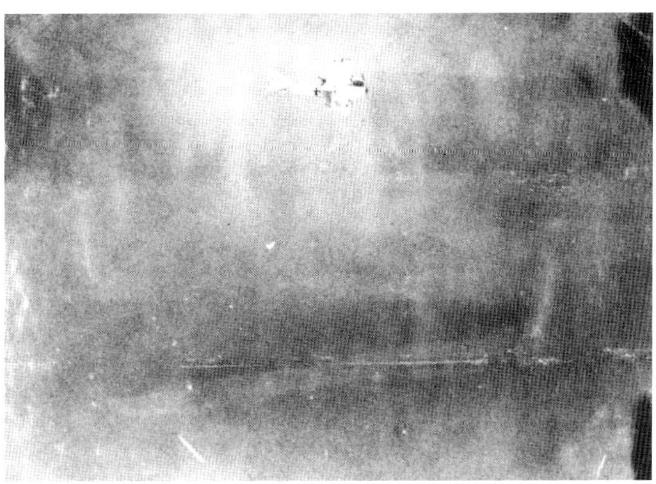

'In the air' is Goering's caption for this shot from the same sequence of 31 March 1916.

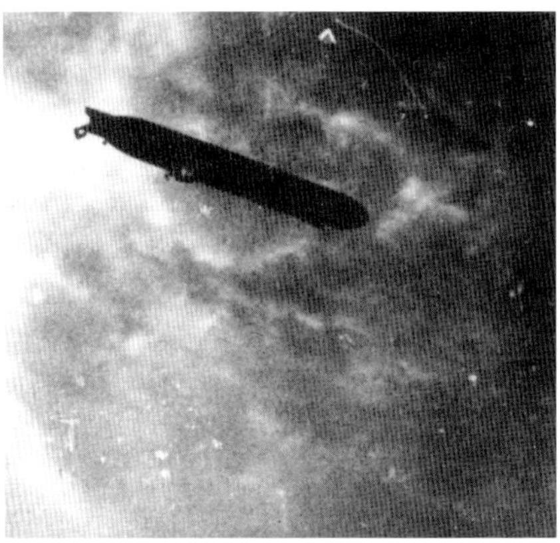

Above: A little difficult to spot, nevertheless, the plane is visible at the center of this aerial shot taken one month later, on 30 April 1916.

Left: Goering's own photograph of a Zeppelin airship in flight overhead.

Below: Goering has captioned this shot 'German Fessel' (balloon).

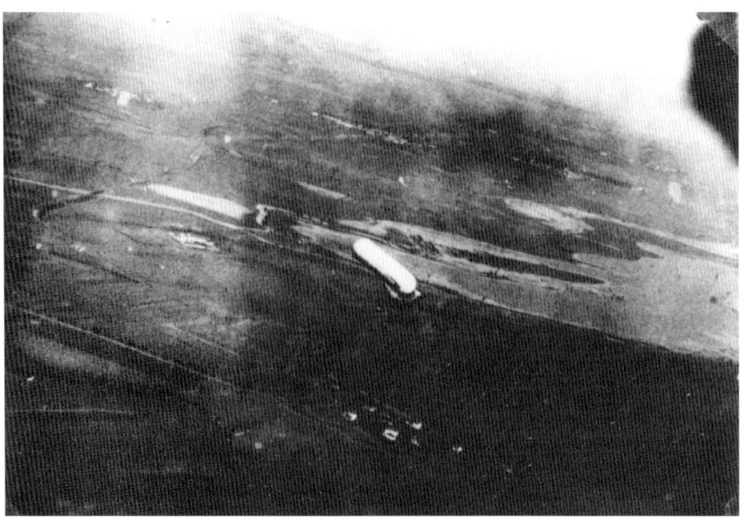

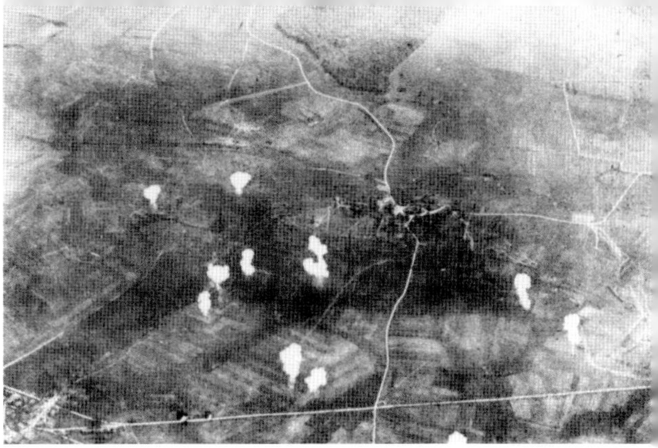

Observer Goering's aerial shot of combat down below, plus the road junction at bottom center of the frame.

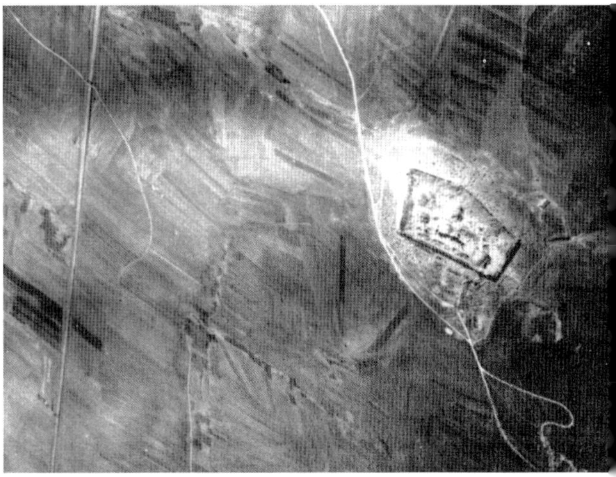

Goering's photo of a French objective, below right. In 1962, Manvell and Fraenkel noted of the mission of 3 June 1915, 'Goering and Lörzer set out alone and without orders to avenge the Crown Princess's honor. Goering shot up a French plane with his pistol and dropped his small but effective bombs (called "airmen's mice") on the sheds of the French airdrome. It was this raid that was said to have inspired him with the idea of carrying an improvised machine gun on the plane. He was the first German airman to do so.'

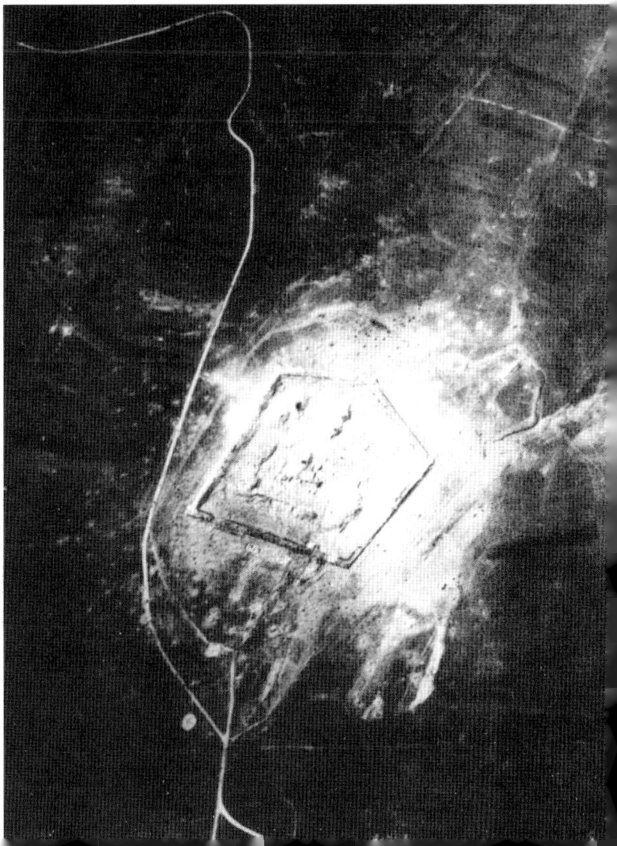

Goering's caption of this aerial photo taken by him is 'Sperrfort [Barricade] Manonviller battered with 42 cm shells, craters are visible.' In 1974, Mosley stated, '[Gen. Erich] von Falkenhayn had a fixation about the French fortress of Verdun ... Each day von Falkenhayn demanded reconnaissance photographs of the Verdun chain [of forts] and such was the concentration of fire inside the walls that they were extremely hard to get. Either the planes were shot down, the cameras smashed, or the results too distant or too blurred. Lörzer and Goering volunteered for the job, and spent three days cruising low over the chain of forts, Lörzer skidding his Albatros, while Goering hung over the side, methodically shooting with his camera.'

Goering captions this simply as 'Lotte', 1916.

Above: Aerial photo taken by Goering, dated 10 or 18 May 1916.

Left: 'Taking skiing lessons in Bayrischzell,' January 1917.

Goering in the rear cockpit with the aircraft's aft machine gun.

The same aircraft as in the previous shot, but this time—and oddly—without the German cross seen on the fuselage in the earlier image.

Captured French Caudron twin-engine biplane, probably the bomber forced down by Goering on 14 March 1916, as we will see later.

'Visit to Metz Airfield', 1915. Three German biplanes are seen at left, and a pair of monoplanes at right. Note the machine gun mounted on the cowling at the far right.

Goering's caption is 'Back from the flight' for this 1915 view of a Fokker single-seat monoplane. Note, too, the cowling-mounted machine gun.

Goering captions this shot, 'Our first plane at the start of the Argonne flight', 22 December 1914. Kilduff states, 'Hermann Goering and Bruno Lörzer made their first combat flight in Aviatik B.II 36/14 (P. 15) from FFA 25's airfield on November 5, 1914.'

German officers pose before an Albatros aircraft.

German aircraft with officers in front.

German aircraft.

'Plane ready to go' is Goering's caption. The aircraft is possibly a Gotha WD.2 reconnaissance plane.

'My GKFZ after air combat', 1916.

Aerial rear machine gunner.

Take-off from a landing strip with hangar at right.

‘At the landing,’ notes Goering of this 1916 scene.

‘The old Prince Heinrich plane’, January 1916. Refers to Kaiser’s younger brother.

'My old plane in Champagne after the crash with another pilot', 1916. The plane is possibly an LVG B.I reconnaissance aircraft.

An idyllic scene of a plane over water.

3

Bruno Lörzer: The Seventh Ace 1891–1960

Authors Lt-Col. John R. Angolia and Clint R. Hackney Jr in their 1984 work *The Pour le Mérite and Germany's First Aces* write:

> Bruno Lörzer finished World War I with a total of 44 victories [exactly *double* that of his friend, Goering], ranking him seventh among the elite of German aces. He was the second most successful fighter pilot, next to Udet, to survive the war.
>
> When Adolf Hitler came to power in 1933, Hermann Goering called upon his old comrade from the Richthofen Squadron and fellow *Pour le Mérite* recipient ... to become the first President of the German Air Sport League, the forerunner of the National Socialist Flying Corps/NSFK.

Who *was* this man, Bruno Lörzer?

> Lörzer was born in Berlin on January 22 1891. Following his graduation from high school, he volunteered for service with the Baden Infantry Regiment No. 112 as a cadet. He attended the Military School at Potsdam, and upon return to his old regiment, was promoted to the rank of lieutenant in January 1913.
>
> He had his first introduction to flying when he was invited to fly with Viktor Stöffler. He was so excited by the experience that he volunteered for service with the German Flying Corps. He was accepted, and quickly assigned to the Flying School at Habsheim. When the war broke out, he was transferred to the school at Frieburg, where he visited another officer of his regiment who was in the hospital ... and during the course of these visits, he influenced his friend—Hermann Goering—to also enter flying.
>
> The two became fast friends. Both went on to become observers in the summer of 1915. Lörzer was then trained as a fighter pilot at the Fokker Works in Schwerin, one of the first German fighter pilots to see action at Verdun. He was then assigned to Boelcke's Squadron, where he learned a great deal from the master. At the end of March 1916, he scored his first victory in aerial combat, followed quickly by a second.
>
> Shortly thereafter, he was seriously wounded, and it was only his skill that enabled him to safely land his aircraft. Upon recovery, he was returned to his squadron at the end of the year.

> In January 1917, he was assigned to the task of forming Fighter Squadron 26. He drew around him such friends as Goering, Walter Blume, and his own younger brother, Fritz. He and his men achieved great success against French and British fighter pilots, especially during the Battle of Flanders.
>
> When Bruno Lörzer earned his twentieth victory, he was awarded the *Pour le Mérite*, followed by appointment to the command of Fighter Squadron 3. Under his command in the spring of 1918 during the Battle of France, the squadron performed exceptionally well. On one day in particular—September 2, 1918—the squadron had numerous engagements, downing a grand total for the day of 26 enemy fighters—all without a single loss to the squadron.
>
> Hindenburg sent Lörzer a telegram congratulating him on his outstanding combat achievements. Two days later—as if to acknowledge the recognition—the squadron brought down yet another eight enemy aircraft ...

In their study *Above the Lines: The Aces and Fighter Units of the German Air Service, Naval Air Service and Flanders Marine Corps, 1914–1918*, Norman L. R. Franks, Frank W. Bailey, and Russell Guest add:

> He was awarded the Iron Cross 2nd Class on March 7, 1915. On the formation of *Jasta 5*, Lörzer joined it, but in late 1916 was posted to *Jasta 17*, then assumed command of *Jasta 26* on January 18, 1917. He would remain associated with this *Jasta* for the rest of the war.
>
> On February 21, 1918, he was given command of Fighter Squadron No. 3, the third of the four main fighter squadrons used by the German Air Service in the war. He usually flew with *Jasta 26* during this period, along with his younger brother, Fritz. Nine days before taking command of *JG 3*, he had been awarded the *Pour le Mérite*, having achieved success in the autumn of 1917 after a very long, slow introduction to the fighter pilot trade.
>
> He was also awarded the Knight's Cross with Swords of the Hohenzollern House Order in late 1917, as well as the Iron Cross 1st Class. In August 1918, JG 3 received BMW-powered Fokker D-7s, and with this superior aircraft, they became the bane of the Royal Air Force, and were quite capable of inflicting heavy casualties right into November 1918, with over 130 kills in September 1918 alone.
>
> He flew a distinctive black-and-white striped aircraft throughout his career. He was promoted to Hauptmann [Captain] on October 10, 1918, and ended the war with 44 victories ...

Among the types of aircraft he shot down throughout the course of his First World War aerial career were Farman, Spad, Nieuport, SE.5A, DH.4, Sopwith Camel and Pup, EA, and BF.2b.

Walter A. Musciano, in his 1965 work *Eagles of the Black Cross*, writes:

> While Bruno Lörzer was the Fuhrer [leader] of *Jasta 26*, he developed ground strafing into a fine art at a time when air-to-ground attacking techniques were in their infancy. If no

enemy aircraft were sighted during a patrol, Lörzer would order the entire *Jasta* to attack trains, trucks, and troop columns, as well as the trenches themselves along the front lines.

The captain continued this policy with his Fighter Squadron 3, and this unit wreaked such havoc behind the Allied lines and at the front that Field Marshal von Hindenburg personally complimented the fighter squadron for its tremendous contribution to the German war effort, and claimed it was worthy of imitation by the remainder of the Air Service.

Lörzer developed his fighter squadron into a formidable fighter unit that exacted a terrific toll of Allied aircraft, especially Spad fighters, during 1918. During September, the fighter squadron destroyed 26 Allied planes without a single loss to themselves ... Despite Bruno Lörzer's outstanding administrative and combat efficiency, he never failed to enjoy himself while on leave, or during the hours devoted to relaxation.

The captain proved to be a most congenial member of any group bent on song or drink, and was very popular and well-liked by the officers and enlisted men alike. He was as well known in the bistros of Berlin as he was at the front ...

Bruno Lörzer ... became an advisor to a German aircraft manufacturer after the war. He remained keenly interested in flying, and won the first German flying contest in a 20 hp light plane. When Goering became Minister of Aviation, Lörzer returned to active service with the rank of colonel, and helped to perfect the technique of combined tank and air attacks that proved so effective in the Second World War ... and was very actively engaged in the drive to train pilots.

By 1938, the ace was a general, and in the following year became commander of the 2nd Flying Corps, thereby controlling a sizeable air fleet that took part in the attacks on Poland and France, as well as in the Battle of Britain.

Bruno Lörzer was also the commanding Luftwaffe general on Sicily, and became Goering's chief of staff [*sic*]. For his service in bringing about the defeat of France, the general was awarded the Knight's Cross of the Iron Cross on May 29, 1940.

After World War II, he was among the German leaders interrogated at a prison camp near Mondorf, Luxembourg. Lörzer was later released, and became a business executive in Germany.

Angolia and Hackney add:

Hermann Goering relied heavily on Lörzer during the formative days of the re-establishment of German aviation as well as the structuring of the new German Air Force. The two men worked closely, with Goering becoming commander-in-chief of the Luftwaffe, and Bruno Lörzer achieving the rank of colonel general, effective February 16, 1943 [after Stalingrad].

Lörzer rose to high rank in the Luftwaffe perhaps due more to his friend Goering than through talent. He was made lieutenant general on December 30, 1939, awarded the World War II Iron Cross 1st Class on September 14, 1939, and then the Knight's Cross of the Iron Cross on May 29, 1940 ...

Lörzer died, aged 69, in Hamburg on 23 August 1960. According to his obituary in *The New York Times* four days later, 'He married the former Else Wulf ... and leaves a daughter, Renate.'

Another interpretation: Goering—fighter ace or cheat?

This is a counterview—in contrast to the previously generally accepted assessment of the 1914–18 partnership between Goering and Lörzer—by writer Hal Giblin, as presented in issue No. 135 of the acclaimed British martial history magazine, *Military Illustrated*:

> When Hermann Goering, former Nazi commander of the Luftwaffe, was struck down by rheumatism on the Western Front, his life changed forever. With his comrade, Bruno Lörzer, he took to the air and became a fighter pilot—but was his reputation as an ace truth or fiction?
>
> The fact that they shared a common parent regiment—Infantry No. 112—brought Hermann Goering and Bruno Lörzer together during their early days in the Imperial German Air Service. Professional soldiers both, they had first met when, as young, newly commissioned military subalterns, they trained with their regiment for the forthcoming European war. The two men came from similar social backgrounds, but from quite different regions of Germany.
>
> Goering—the fourth child and second son of Dr. Heinrich Ernst and Franziska ('Fanny') Goering—was born in the Upper Bayern district of Bavaria on January 12, 1893. Following a conventional education, young Hermann decided he would like to pursue a military career, and at the age of 19 received a cadet commission on June 22, 1912. After completing an 18-month course at the Main Cadet Institute, he joined Infantry Regiment No. 112—a 'local' Bavarian unit.
>
> When the war came in August 1914, Goering commanded a platoon as his regiment (8/112) advanced into the Vosges region in France. At first, the new war was one of fluidity and movement, and Goering's regiment helped to push back the French Army at Lothringen, Nancy-Epinal, and Flirey.
>
> The first of Hermann Goering's many decorations—the Iron Cross 2nd Class—was awarded on September 15, 1914, for his services as an infantry officer. In the same month—following weeks of rigorous campaigning—he was struck down and sent home to be hospitalized in Freiburg with a most unexpected malady for a young, active man—a severe attack of rheumatism.
>
> Surprised by the debilitating severity of the ailment, Goering was forced to rethink his future. Still intent on a military career—but uncomfortably aware that his physical defects could sidetrack him into a chair-borne commissary role—he began seriously to consider the alternatives.
>
> Whilst attending the hospital in Freiburg to see an injured comrade, Bruno Lörzer—then an observer in the Flying Service—noticed that a former colleague from his old regiment, none other than Hermann Goering—was also confined there, and took the opportunity to visit his sickbed.

Inevitably, they discussed the new Flying Service that Goering was quick to see the possibility of a deliverance from his dilemma. His prompt application for transfer to the Flying Service was soon approved, and he was posted to *Feldflieger Abteilung* [Field Aviation Unit] 3 before going on to FA 25 as a probationary observer on October 28, 1914.

Before long, he was flying operationally in the Argonne region of France, where he again met Lörzer. During the winter months of 1914-15, the two flew many reconnaissance flights over the opposing German and French lines. Lörzer gained his first award in March 1915, when he received the Iron Cross 2nd Class.

In the same month, Hermann Goering was given the Iron Cross 1st Class to add to the 2nd Class of the same order he had won as an infantry officer in September 1914.

Bruno Lörzer—two years older than Goering—was born in Berlin on January 22, 1891. After completing his education, he applied for a cadet commission, and was attached to Infantry Regiment No. 112. An 18-month course at the Cadet School in Potsdam followed, and, after successfully graduating, he was allowed to rejoin his regiment in 1913 with the rank of lieutenant.

A more or less casual invitation to fly with German aviation pioneer and Schneider Trophy contestant Viktor Stöffler had a dramatic impact on the young Lörzer who, subsequently, would not rest content until his reactive application to join the relatively new Flying Service was approved.

He trained first at the Flying School at Habsheim, but when war broke out in August 1914, he was transferred to the school at Freiburg, and it was at the military hospital in that town that he persuaded Hermann Goering to follow him into aviation.

Late in June 1915, Lörzer left FA 25 and Goering behind, to fly with FA 60 and FAA 203, before going on to serve with KEK (short for *Kampfeinsitzer-Kommando*) at Jametz as a fighter pilot. On March 21, 1916, he gained the first of his 44 victories, bringing down a Farman over Fosse Wood. His second victory followed 10 days later.

His considerable ability was soon recognized, and he was one of a small, elite group sent to join the Scout Squadrons being formed by the peerless Oswald Boelcke. A brief, uneventful period with *Jasta 5* (Royal Prussian) was followed by a transfer to *Jasta 17* (Royal Prussian) late in 1916. An appointment as commanding officer of the recently created *Jasta 26* (Royal Prussian) came on January 18, 1917.

Operating above Flanders (Belgium) and Northern France, *Jasta 26* and its commanding officer, Bruno Lörzer, enjoyed initially slow but increasingly compounding success—mainly against the (British) Royal Flying Corps. Sporting their distinctive squadron markings of black and white fuselage bands, they took off on their first battle flight on January 27, 1917, and gained their first victory a month later on February 25th.

By the time the unit had achieved its 100th victory in December 1917, it had occupied airfields at Colmar-Nord, Habsheim, Guise-Ost, Bohain-Nord, Iseghem, Abeele, Bavichove, and Markebeke—remarkable testament to the mobility and organizational expertise of the German Air Service at this time.

On February 12, 1918—with 22 victories to his personal credit—Bruno Lörzer received the ultimate accolade of the *Pour le Mérite*, the 'Blue Max', to add to the Iron Cross 1st Class and the Knight's Cross with Swords of the Hohenzollern House Order he had received in 1917.

Nine days later, he was appointed to command the newly formed *Jagdgeschwader* [Fighter Group] 111, the third of four main scout/fighter plane *geschwadern* employed in the service of the Kaiser's air arm during the Great War. *JG 111* consisted of four fighter 'squadrons'—all Royal Prussian—*Jasta 2* (the elite, 'Boelcke' *Jasta*—then commanded by Karl Bolle); *Jasta 26* (Bruno's brother Fritz was brought from *Jasta 6* to succeed him as commanding officer); *Jasta 27* (led by Hermann Goering), and *Jasta 36* (Heinrich Bongartz commanding).

A formidable force that became even more so when—in August 1918—they were equipped with state-of-the-art Fokker D.VIIs powered by BMW [Bavarian Motor Works] engines. These nimble biplanes accounted for no less than 130 Royal Air Force machines during the month of September 1918 alone.

Indeed, on September 2nd—during the course of a very busy day—*JG 111* shot down 26 Allied aircraft (Bruno Lörzer—not to be left out—got a Camel over Dury), duly receiving a congratulatory telegram from the supreme commander, von Hindenburg, for their efforts. Thankfully for the Allies, the end of the war was imminent.

Throughout this period of his *JG 111* command, Bruno Lörzer retained his 'signature' black and white striping on personal machines, and chose to continue to fly mainly with his old *Jasta 26*, now commanded by his brother, Fritz. Fritz Lörzer had a personal score of seven victories when he took over *Jasta 26* on February 21, 1918, and went on to record another four kills before he was sent down himself—a wing breaking under the stress of a searing combat turn—and taken prisoner on June 12, 1918.

Instinctively aggressive and always restless, Lörzer never allowed the men and machines under his command the luxury of idle moments. Whenever there was a lull in aerial activity, he encouraged the ground strafing of enemy troops and transport, developing—in the process—innovatory techniques in this brand-new area of warfare, techniques that would wreak particular havoc on Allied ground forces during the final advance.

Bruno Lörzer—promoted to *Hauptmann* on October 10, 1918—finished the war with a total of 44 victories. With so many other surviving German ex-servicemen, he returned to a shambolic, broken down, disaffected society, ripe for revolution.

Goering—left behind with the ponderous two- and three-seat machines of FA 25 when Lörzer moved on to flying fighter planes—quickly decided he had better follow his friend's lead. His first priority was to qualify as a pilot, and so he left the combat zone for the Freiburg Flying School in June 1915.

In July—with his pilot training in full swing—he was understandably gratified to discover that his own State of Bavaria had awarded him the Order of the Zahringer Lion for his services as an observer with FA 25. Having finally satisfied the examiners in September 1915, Goering was sent first to Army Flying Park No. 5 before returning to his old unit at the beginning of the following month.

Hermann Goering's first 'confirmed' victory was achieved—supposedly—over a French Farman at 2.30 PM on November 15, 1915, although, in fact, the French lost no machines on that day! This [was] the first of a disturbing number of 'phantom' victories claimed by—and attributed to—Hermann Goering.

The Imperial German Air Service was rightly credited with having a strict and exacting confirmation procedure—probably the most precise of any of the flying services on both sides of the conflict—but despite these undoubtedly high standards, too many of Goering's claims remain inadequately founded, defying close scrutiny: early evidence, perhaps, of the devious, ambitiously forceful, and ruthlessly self-glorifying personality that would fully emerge in later life.

Following a period in hospital recovering from a knee injury sustained in a crash in Germany, the early weeks of 1916 saw Goering involved in a heavy flying schedule preceding the German attack on Verdun, piloting not only the Albatros two-seaters but also the very large, twin-engine, three-seat AEG G.IIs.

Goering was almost constantly in action throughout the spring and early summer and, by July, had begun flying a single-seat Halberstadt D.III from his base at Stenay (France). Temporary transfer to Jametz and the single-seat unit—FAA 203—followed, but by August, he had returned to FA 25, this time to pilot single-seats exclusively.

Within weeks, FA 25 was disbanded, and Goering was sent to the *Kampfstaffel* (Fighting Section) at Metz [in French (later German) Alsace-Lorraine]. By now, the crack *Jagdstaffeln* had been introduced, and he was posted, briefly, to *Jasta 7* in company with his longtime friend, Bruno Lörzer.

In September 1916—with the Somme battles raging—Goering joined *Jasta 5* at Gonnelieu, southwest of Cambrai. On November 2, 1916, he received a hip wound during an aerial combat, spending weeks in hospital, first in France and then back home in Germany.

Enjoying a week of leave in January 1917—just prior to a return to full duty—he visited Bruno Lörzer's new command, *Jasta 26*. No doubt by 'pulling the appropriate strings', Goering wangled himself a posting to *Jasta 26* on February 15, 1917.

Piloting an Albatros D.III, he scored steadily, if not spectacularly, and by May 17, 1917, with seven 'victories' to his credit, he was rather surprisingly given his own command as *Staffelführer* (Section Leader) of *Jasta 27*. He was, it must be remembered, a professional soldier with five years' service, much of it in combat, but still there were many who thought that there were others better qualified than he, who should have been preferred.

Goering's new command was stationed at Ghistelles, behind the German lines facing the Ypres (Belgium) salient. Formed three months earlier, *Jasta 27* had still to record its first success when Hermann Goering took over. Having insisted on bringing his favorite Albatros (2049/16) with him, Goering lost time in leading his *Jasta* against the enemy air forces.

It was, however, nearly three weeks before his *Jasta* registered its first 'hit'. Their second success on June 8, 1917—a (French) Nieuport XVII belonging to Squadron I—was, perhaps inevitably, credited to the *Staffelführer* himself (his 8th.)

The war ground on into 1918, and shortly after registering his 17th victory on February 21st of that year (a combat he would later describe in an article for a 1933 edition of *Popular Flying*, a British aviation magazine edited by the 'Biggles' creator, Capt. W. E. Johns), Goering fell ill with a severe attack of tonsillitis, spending several weeks in hospital.

He returned in time to organize his *Jasta*'s move to Erchin as part of the German Army's elaborate preparations for the launch of its spring offensive scheduled for March 21, 1918. As *Jasta 27* settled into its new base southwest of Douai, Fokker triplanes arrived to replace their older machines.

The Fokkers were kept extremely busy throughout the March Offensive (codenamed the *Kaiserschlacht* (Kaiser's Battle), but the *Staffelführer*, personally, had to wait a full 17 days into the battle before he could claim a further victory, his 18th.

Yet another of the slightly odd circumstances that punctuated Hermann Goering's Great War career was the timing of his *Pour le Mérite*/'Blue Max' award. As the air war—and its attendant technology—developed and changed, so, too, did the threshold criteria of the number of victories needed for even consideration to be given for the award of the 'Blue Max'.

Initially, eight victories were enough, but as more and more pilots qualified, this was soon doubled to 16 and, by the middle of 1917, the requirement had been raised to at least 20—20 officially confirmed victories, that is.

Goering—who by then already held the prerequisite Knight's Cross with Swords of the Royal Hohenzollern House Order, as well as his own State of Bavaria's Military Karl-Friedrich Merit Order—received his *Pour le Mérite* with just 18 confirmed victories on June 2, 1918.

Celebrations subsequent upon the announcement of the *Staffelführer*'s 'Blue Max' were curtailed, as *Jasta 27* moved its base on the following day to a new aerodrome opposite the French front at Mont de Soissons Ferme.

After the Red Baron's death on April 21, 1918, the command of *Jagdgeschwader 1* (Richthofen) had passed to Capt. Wilhelm Reinhard. Now, Reinhard, too, was dead, killed on July 3, 1918 at Aldersdorf on the outskirts of Berlin, test flying a new Dornier design, the Zeppelin-Lindau D1.

Coincidentally, Goering had also been present at the tests, and witnessed Reinhard's death crash. Goering, like Reinhard, had been ordered to Berlin to test and offer his opinion of the new machine. He had taken Z-L D1 up over Aldersdorf and put it through its paces in front of an extremely distinguished audience assembled for the occasion.

He landed to make his report as Reinhard took off to make his own evaluation. Unfortunately, as Reinhard dived and spun, a strut snapped and the top wing crumbled and collapsed, allowing the pilot no chance of recovery.

Just over a week later—on July 11, 1918, with three more claimed victories against the French under his belt—Goering was suddenly and unexpectedly summoned to headquarters.

Again to the surprise—and even the chagrin of many of his contemporaries—Goering was appointed to command the internationally famous *JG 1*, the Richthofen 'Wing'. Perhaps his cool—and overtly successful—handling of the Zeppelin-Lindau D1 at Aldersdorf, together with the undoubted force of his personality and supreme self-confidence, had impressed senior officers present at the Berlin trials.

Certainly, there were others more qualified to succeed to this most prestigious of appointments, but the Goering 'luck' held good, yet again!

Goering claimed just one more victory—his 22nd—before the end of the war. When the end came with the devastating news of the Kaiser's abdication on November 10, 1918, Goering's last act of defiance—with the help of his four *Staffelführern*—was to ensure that his remaining Fokkers did not (contrary to orders) pass intact into Allied hands.

Hermann Goering and Bruno Lörzer—the once raw, gauche, prewar infantry subalterns—had both risen to command elite aviation units—a possibility that could never have even occurred to them in 1913.

They both were recipients of the highest military honors their states could confer upon them. Now both had to return to a defeated, disaffected, and Kaiser-less country—their wartime successes largely meaningless and irrelevant.

The two men kept in touch, but each went their separate ways. While Hermann Goering immersed himself in politics, Lörzer became an advisor to the aviation industry. In 1933—after the National Socialists/Nazis came to power—Hitler appointed Goering as Reich Commissioner for Air.

Now politically trustworthy friends would be needed to fill key roles in the administration. For the Luftwaffe—the Third Reich's emerging air service—who better than old comrade and friend, Bruno Lörzer? Lörzer re-entered service with the rank of *Oberst* [Colonel].

Drawing upon some of the ground strafing experiences he had in the last months of the Great War, Lörzer headed a team perfecting techniques of combined tank and aircraft attacks—tactics that would be used to great effect in 1939 and after.

Lörzer was also appointed President of the so-called German Air Sport League, and was active in recruiting and training pilots. Promoted to general in 1938, and in the following year appointed commander of the 2nd Flying Corps, Lörzer played his part in the invasions of Poland and France (for which he was awarded the Knight's Cross of the Iron Cross) and, less successfully, in the Battle of Britain.

Later in the war, he commanded the Luftwaffe in Sicily, and became Goering's Chief of Staff [*sic*]. Captured by the Allies at the war's end, he was eventually released, and became a business executive in Germany before his death on August 22, 1960, age of 69.

Another view of Lörzer as Goering's 'Best Friend Forever'

In January 2010, I read the diary entry for 25 April 1945 of the last Luftwaffe Chief of General Staff, Col. Gen. Karl Koller, concerning the aftermath of the earlier arrest by the SS of Reich Marshal Hermann Goering on the Obersalzberg in Bavaria on Hitler's orders. Gen. Koller was also under arrest by the SS:

> Gen. Lörzer appears in civilian clothes, sneaking in through the back door in the kitchen. Asks about the Reich Marshal, and whether he could do anything for him, then leaves the house again the same way. That one is afraid that somebody might notice him calling on me. He promised to come back every day.
>
> Lörzer never came back. A few days later ... I heard that Lörzer—together with State Secretary [Paul 'Pilli'] Korner—left Berchtesgaden in a car at top speed immediately after his visit to me ... That's the man who the Reich Marshal thought was his best friend, and for whom he stood up time and again although this brought the Führer's wrath down on him.

On 2 May 1945, Koller added a final entry:

> Lörzer and Korner together left the staff office in a car for the Tengelmann estate somewhere along the Autobahn [highway]. They are said to have taken 70 fully packed cases with them [the contents of which were—and still are—unknown].

To be fair to Lörzer, one must ask what he could have done—led Luftwaffe troops against the SS for a man whom Hitler had fired, and also declared a national traitor? In addition, Lörzer and everyone else knew what had happened to the top SA leadership during the 'Night of the Long Knives' in the summer of 1934: mass executions without any sort of trial whatsoever. This was what Goering himself feared in April 1945, and he had good reason, too, as Martin Bormann in Berlin wanted Goering shot, but Hitler refused.

Goering's fellow fighter pilot and 'Blue Max' recipient Capt. Bruno Lörzer (1891–1960), seen here in a popular picture postcard wearing his 'Max' at the throat, the Iron Cross ribbon at left, and the actual Iron Cross (top) and German Flying Service Pilot/Observer's Badge at bottom, both at right. It was Bruno Lörzer who paved the way for Goering's career as an airman—first by taking him aboard as his observer, and later by way of saving his life during aerial combat. Lörzer finished the First World War with a total of forty-four victories, ranking him seventh among the elite of German aces. He was the second most successful fighter pilot, next to Udet, to survive the war, according to authors Angolia and Hackney.

Goering's caption is 'Nap in our apartment', indicating that he (left) and Lörzer (right) roomed together. Note the close 'wiffle' haircut common to all modern armies. The site is Stenay, 1914.

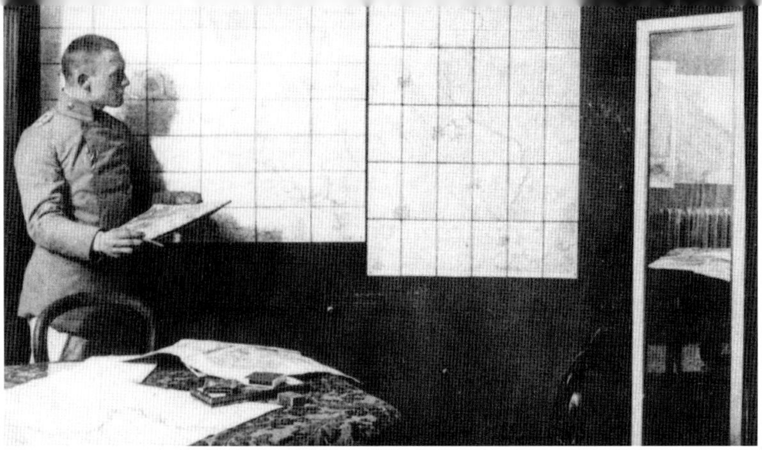

Goering in the Stenay headquarters map room in 1914.

Above: In the same triad of 1914 views of Goering, here he is seen studying a map at Stenay.

Left: Goering's caption reads, 'Lörzer [right] and Frau von der Osten in plane'.

Of this picture, Kilduff notes, 'Hermann Goering and Bruno Lörzer made their first combat flight in Aviatik B.II 36/14 from FFA 25's airfield on November 5, 1914.'

Goering stands with arms akimbo (left) with Lörzer (right) with their Rumpler observation plane, in June 1915, as they appeared in another much published view of their combat service together.

A second photo of the same site, plane, and location in June 1915. Goering's caption—as written in ink at the bottom—is 'Officers of the FFL. Abt. 25'. Goering shields his eyes from the sun at left as Lörzer stands immediately to his left. The other men are unknown to me.

Lörzer (left) and Goering (right) in 1914.

'Our great aircraft at 2,500 meters high, 1916', reads Goering's caption.

Goering's caption reads, 'In the air, 1916'.

Above left: 'Director Bassler [civilian clothes at center] and Schaesberg [top, with machine guns] before my new plane', 1916.

Above right: Goering wearing summer white uniform tunic, hands in pocket. Note the Iron Cross at mid-right.

Lörzer at his desk.

Goering (right) and Lörzer (left) on the same occasion.

Goering (far left, seated) and Lörzer (third from left), both in summer whites, enjoying a meal with other officers. Note the presence of Goering's cane—no affectation, that—because he needed it due to his rheumatism.

Kilduff notes of this photo, 'Despite worsening experiences with Fokker Eindeckers, FFA 25 retained two, which Goering photographed with a small personal camera, as seen here.'

Suited up for flight, Lörzer (right) appears with an unknown officer in front of a Fokker Eindecker (monoplane) as a backdrop.

Goering's caption reads, '1st Lt Parschau [center] tries the early Pfalz Eindecker', 1916. Note, too, the fixed Spandau machine gun on the top of the cowling at left.

'Lörzer starts with his Fokker,' Goering wrote of this photo in 1916. Author Walter A. Musciano notes, 'By the end of March 1916, Lörzer had two victories. In the following month, he was so badly wounded that he was not able to return to the front until the fall of 1916. During this episode, Bruno fought unconsciousness due to loss of blood and was fortunate to sight his airfield. He managed to land his tricky Eindecker before he slumped over in the cockpit. Oswald Boelcke was the first to reach the wounded pilot, and lifted an unconscious Lörzer from the cockpit himself.'

Goering's caption for this 1917 aerial shot is 'Eindecker in flight'.

Above: Of this photo, Kilduff has written, 'Goering's camera also recorded Bruno Lörzer's Eindecker crash in July 1916.' Goering did not take the photo himself, because he is sitting in the cockpit wearing his black leather helmet. Note, too, the brace of fixed Spandau machine guns on the cowling at left.

Left: A recuperating Bruno Lörzer (left) is visited by Goering at right, 1916. Goering's caption reads, 'We two together'.

On the same occasion in 1916, Goering (left) and Lörzer (right) are joined by their friend, Assistant Dr Gimbel (center).

Above left: 'Lörzer [second from left] with Turkish colonel [center] at the airfield, October 1916,' is Goering's caption. Another Turkish officer appears at far right, conversing with a German officer to his right, while yet another German officer is at the far left.

Above right: Goering's caption reads, 'Lörzer in Bohain, 1917'.

Above left: 'Bruno and his machine, 1917'.

Above right: A trim Lörzer standing at parade rest, a position known to soldiers the world over.

'Nap at Habsheim, 1917'. Lörzer is at center.

'Sunbathing in Klubkessel,' Goering wrote of this 1917 shot, possibly in the same sequence as the previous picture.

Goering's picture of Lörzer off duty, cradling a pair of snow skis in the crook of his right arm, 1917.

'On the balcony', 1917 photo of Goering by Lörzer, probably on the same site and occasion as the previous picture.

Above left: Of this photo, Hal Giblin has written, 'Early days. Both men [Lörzer, left, and Goering at right] wear the ribbon of the Iron Cross 2nd Class, the insignia of the Iron Cross 1st Class and their Pilot's Badges on field gray uniforms with high red collars.' The picture is published here full frame for the very first time, however.

Above right: Goering with his cane and goggles at left poses with his friend Lörzer at right in a photo that I first published in 1994 in a magazine format. This is its first book format publication, however.

Goering (left) and another officer (possibly Lörzer) walking together on a wartime airfield.

(Left to right) Lörzer, Goering, and Wusthoff with a pair of friendly nurses.

Above left: Goering, seated at right on the bench, captions this, 'Parting photo of Jagdstaffel [Fighter Section] 26,' 1917. Lörzer is at the bench at center.

Above right: The brothers Lörzer, fighter pilots both, with Bruno at left and Fritz at right. Note that Fritz also wears both the Iron Cross and the Pilot/Observer's Badge on his tunic.

The brothers Lörzer and their mates played host to a captured British airman (at center on the bottom step). Both sides practiced this unique code of chivalry between rival fliers in the Great War, fêting their downed opposite numbers with food and drink until they were taken away by the Army into more mundane PoW captivity. Bruno stands at the left on the bottom step and Fritz on the right on the landing above, just over the right arm of the captured pilot.

Above left: Kilduff notes of this view, 'New Iron Cross 1st Class recipients Goering [left] and Lörzer [right] were congratulated by FFA 25's resident physician Dr Gimbel [at center, with tipped swagger stick].' This, however, is the full frame of that shot, here published for the first time, top to bottom. Note Goering's wristwatch on his left arm, as well as the photo of the unknown woman. In his right hand, he also carries his cane once again.

Above right: Goering's caption reads, 'Vizefeldw. [Sgt Maj.] Lörzer, Kette [Group] I,' 1917.

Left: Of this photo, Hal Giblin has written, 'Goering, commanding *Jasta* 27, [left, again with cane] and Lörzer, commanding *Jasta* 26, briefly shared the same home field in 1917. They pose in front of an Albatros D.III.'

Below: Bruno Lörzer's Albatros D.Va. The number is 2299, as seen on its tail fin at far left, with pilot Bruno Lörzer at right. Note also the four album cornices at each corner of this photo!

Above left: German Army Field Marshal Paul von Hindenburg—seen here in a Great War portrait—reportedly sent Bruno Lörzer a telegram congratulating him on strafing the Allied enemy on the ground in 1918.

Above right: Another well-known photo of Goering (left) and Lörzer (right) in 1918, with Fokker works official Friedrich Seekatz standing between them. The war's end at this point was but a few months distant. Note Goering's puttees. According to authors Ewan Butler and Gordon Young in their 1951 biography of Goering, 'All that winter [1916], Goering and Lörzer flew together, and on one occasion at least, Lörzer saved his friend's life by forcing down a French fighter that would have otherwise inevitably destroyed him [Goering], but by now the pupil had overtaken the master.'

A rather well-known view of three famous aviators, *from left to right:* Lörzer, Dutch designer Anthony Fokker, and Goering, 1918. The two German airmen proudly wear their 'Blue Max' decorations at the throat.

4

Goering from Fighter Pilot to Final Commander of the 'Flying Circus' 1915–18

The year was 1918. The third and last commander of the famed Richthofen 'Flying Circus' was about to take over the unit in German-occupied France. Writing in 1974, Mosley described the scene vividly:

> That morning of July 14th, Hermann Goering probably had only one friend in *JG Richthofen 1*, and that was its adjutant, Lt Karl Bodenschatz.
>
> He had taken to the new commander right from their first meeting, and it was an admiration that was to last a lifetime. 'A man of personal charm, but underneath, I suspect, he is a tough customer,' he wrote shortly afterwards. 'You could see it in the way he moved, and the way he talked ...'

In his otherwise authoritative book about First World War fliers *The Great Air War*, Aaron Norman says of that first meeting of the Richthofen 'Flying Circus' and its new commander:

> He then delivered his introductory speech. He told them—these veterans and victory-rich aces—what they had been doing wrong. Then he told them how he was going to institute the necessary reforms. The old order was changing, and the new—as outlined by Goering—was not to the liking of his audience.

Mosley disputes this account:

> This is far from being a fair or an accurate account of what happened. Hermann Goering was no fool, and was now 25 years old. He had just been given command of the most prestigious group of fliers in the world, and he knew he could never make a success of the job without their willing and devoted co-operation.
>
> Nothing was more likely to lose it from the start than to begin the new regime by berating them. Changes would come later, but, for the moment, it was necessary to win their confidence.
>
> He walked onto the briefing platform followed by Bodenschatz and by a junior pilot of the squadron, who, by tradition, had been chosen to introduce him to his comrades.

> Lt von Wedel was nervous, and he muffed his prepared speech, so that a restless murmur passed through the throng of pilots.
>
> Then Bodenschatz stepped forward and handed over to Goering the *Geschwaderstock*, the blackthorn unit walking stick that had been made by a Bavarian craftsman and presented to von Richthofen ... Now Goering took it in his hands and balanced it tenderly, as if the symbol of majesty had now been passed on to him. He paused and stared down at the fliers with his piercing blue eyes, and waited until there was silence, and then he said:
>
> 'Gentlemen, let me say at once what a great and special honour has been done to me by His Imperial Majesty in making me commander of this illustrious squadron! Great battles have been fought, and great men have died to make it so. I am only too sensible of the fact that there are no better fliers in the world than those I see before me now.
>
> 'I hope I shall be worthy of your confidence and your trust. I hope you will continue to be worthy of those of your comrades who have given their lives for you, for the Air Force, and for Germany. We will need to give of our best, all of us, for there are grave times ahead. We will face them together for the glory of the Fatherland!'
>
> It was simple, and it was spoken with the utmost gravity, and the pilots were impressed. 'The new commander has got off to a good start,' Bodenschatz noted in his diary.

Hermann Goering's road to his last and most famous posting of the First World War—and one, moreover, that was to propel him to a top leadership position in Adolf Hitler's Nazi Party afterwards—began in 1915, when he decided to abandon his role as merely a flying observer for that of a pursuit pilot in aerial combat with Allied opponents.

Here is how it all happened.

According to Mosley:

> It was inevitable that Hermann Goering should become a pilot ... He was always a man of great enthusiasms, but the moment he had squeezed a new game or a new métier dry of its possibilities, he needed to pass on to new adventures. For a time—as the famed Flying Trapezist in the observer's seat—he had been the talk of every aircraft mess along the Western Front, but now—with new and dangerous forms of air war developing—it was the fighter pilot who was becoming the hero of the day ...
>
> Goering longed to see his name included with them. In June 1915, he arrived in Freiburg to begin a course as a pilot, and not for the first time in his life, he excelled all the rest. He made perfect takeoffs and landings almost from the start (not unnaturally, since he had seen Lörzer do them often enough) and, once in the air, speedily showed an aptitude for aerobatics that impressed his instructors, and turned his fellow pupils green with envy.
>
> He was afterwards to boast that he was the only one to emerge from the course with an absolutely clean record, never having crashed a plane from start to finish.

Of this period, British authors Butler and Young state:

> Although the aircraft in which he flew over the rolling hills of the Black Forest were crazy, slow contraptions by the standards of even 10 years later, they were still—in

1915—among the finest fighting aeroplanes in the world, and their pilots members of a minutely small elite among the warring nations, an elite, moreover, that sought, on both sides, to keep alive traditions of chivalry that some of the groundlings, bogged down in Flanders mud, were beginning to forget.

Goering displayed traits in his character that are more often found allied in men of his race than in those of any other—a muddled idealism based on a patriotism equally confused, a rather mawkish sentimentality, and a ruthlessness in action that could and did—when necessary—dominate his whole personality.

By the autumn of 1915, Goering was a trained pilot, back at the front with the faithful Lörzer as a member of *5 Abteilung* [Section].

His return to active service coincided with the autumn offensive of the French and British armies, and the division was kept busy enough with its own reconnaissance duties, and with the interception of enemy aircraft entrusted with similar missions over the German lines.

Manvell and Fraenkel add:

He gained his wings in record time ... In October 1915, he became a '*Jagdflieger* (pursuit flier)' or fighter pilot. Goering and Lörzer were members of *Jagdstaffel* (Fighter Section) 5, a section of the new armada of twin-engine fighter planes that Germany was putting into the air on the Western Front.

Frischauer writes:

Courses were short and intense, but he passed his final tests easily, returned quickly to the front, and rejoined his unit, this time on equal terms with his old friend Lörzer. At first, they both still flew the big AEG type of plane, but they soon 'organized' the coveted transfer to a fighter detachment—Squadron 5. Side by side, the two lieutenants threw themselves into the fight. Goering still a little uncertain, always over-ambitious, often incautious, sometimes not only risking his life, but his valuable aircraft, quite unnecessarily.

The older and more experienced Lörzer—a man with a calmer temperament—was often forced to dash to the rescue of his young comrade. Many prominent air officers of the Second World War who worshipped Goering were highly critical of his decision to appoint Lörzer to a key post in the Luftwaffe.

That Goering would not have become an airman without Lörzer's help was an open secret, but few of his critics realized that the Reich Marshal and commander-in-chief of the Luftwaffe owed his very life to Lörzer. Hermann Goering would not have survived his first air battles in the French skies had it not been for his faithful friend.

In 1989, Irving asserted:

The legend has it that he took flying lessons at his own expense, but ... the personnel file is more mundane. It shows that he was posted to the flying training school at Freiburg (where he first met Lörzer) at the end of June 1915, and returned to the 5th Army in mid-September. He flew his first operational sortie as a fighter pilot on the third day of

> October—a 140-minute patrol after which he nonchalantly wrote in his report that he had, 'fought off seven French planes one after the other'.
>
> The planes were primitive, the pilots daredevils and gladiators; their life expectancy was not long, but if they shot down an enemy officer, the man might be dined for days afterward in the German messes. There was a chivalry toward a defeated foe then that did not recur in other arenas, or in later wars.
>
> On November 16, 1915, Goering was credited with his first official 'kill', a Farman shot down at Tahure. For the 5th Army's great assault on Verdun that finally began three months later, he flew fighter G.49, one of the big, 300 hp AEG planes. In this fast, heavily armed fighter, with its superior rate of climb, he shot down a French [Caudron] bomber on March 14, 1916.
>
> His observer's action report reads: 'Air battle with three big French warplanes, Caudrons. After 15 minutes managed to shoot down one ... It went down toward the French lines in a steep glide, with its port engine on fire, and Lt Goering giving chase, we managed to force it to land behind our lines [south-east edge of Haumont Woods]. We circled overhead at 150 feet until we observed them taken prisoner ... Their plane had about a dozen hits. The crew, an officer and a sergeant, were both uninjured.'

But this is getting ahead of our story a bit. According to Butler and Young in *Marshal Without Glory*:

> How many of the stories of Goering's wartime exploits subsequently related by diligent Nazi writers were historically correct is a matter for conjecture. One of the many tales told in Goering's heyday is of a reconnaissance sortie that he is said to have made with two other fighters on a misty day in November [1915]. They were flying at 2,000 feet when Goering observed ahead—well behind the British lines—a Handley Page bomber of monstrous size.
>
> This British aircraft had only just been brought into service, and while the officers of No. 5 Division had discussed what little was known about it, none of them had hitherto seen an actual machine. Goering determined to destroy this great bomber. So intent was Goering on the prey that lay ahead, that he failed to observe that he was alone. Less single minded than he, the pilots of the two machines that had kept him company perceived—1,500 feet above them—at least 20 British fighters, and had prudently made course for the German lines.
>
> Goering had eyes only for the giant bomber. Swooping down on it, he killed the rear gunner, climbed, swooped again, and put the forward machine gun out of action. A third burst from his gun set fire to one of the enemy's two engines, and the bomber began to spiral downwards. Only then did the hunter hear the roar of the British Sopwiths on his tail, and see that a dozen of them were diving to the attack.
>
> A burst of fire holed Goering's petrol tank—and as he set his hand to the cock that controlled the reserve supply of fuel—another burst ripped the fabric of his wings to shreds, and grazed his right leg and hip.
>
> There was nothing for it but a hazardous nose dive, in the hope that it might still be possible to pull out of it 3,400 feet from the ground. The German pilot jerked down the nose of his aircraft as the British fighters almost jostled one another to pursue him, and impeded each other in doing so.

> The fighter still answered to the controls. With petrol streaming from his punctured tank, Goering hedge-hopped across the German lines and somehow landed in a graveyard, whose church had been converted by the Germans into a field hospital. Within a minute or two of landing, Goering was on the operating table in the crypt. His aircraft carried more than 60 bullet holes. The graze to the leg was no more than a flesh wound, but the bullet that had hit Goering in the hip had done more serious damage, and left behind it a scar, 10 inches long, that he carried for the rest of his days.

Did the Handley Page combat actually take place? Biographers Mosley, Frischauer, and Manvell and Fraenkel all treat the incident as if it did. Irving rejoins:

> On June 20, 1916, he was given a new Halberstadt plane, D 115. He had been comfortable at Stenay Airfield—he pasted into his album pictures of himself at his well-appointed writing desk and even better appointed dressing table—but from July 9th, he flew sorties from Metz over the 3rd Army's front.
>
> A typical action report six days later records four missions by him: in one dogfight over Cote Claire, he fired five rounds into an enemy Voisin, killing the observer, then lost his quarry as it plunged into the clouds. Gradually, his score increased, although some claims were disallowed. 'I regret,' wrote the lieutenant colonel commanding the 5th Army's air element, 'that I am unable to credit to Lt Goering the plane shot down on July 24th.' He was, however, credited with a twin-engine Caudron destroyed at Mameg on the 30th (his third kill).
>
> For three months after that, the Goering file recorded only a series of new postings—back to 25 Field Air Detachment, then back again to *Kampfstaffel* [Fighter Section] Metz, and three weeks after that, on September 28th, to 7th Fighter Section.
>
> Bored as the fighting stagnated, he asked to be posted to 5th Fighter Squadron; the Crown Prince gave permission, and on October 20th, again with his buddy Lörzer, Goering made the transfer. Here he flew mainly escort duty for bombers until his luck ran out, on November 2, 1916 [as we have seen].
>
> 'Plane in need of repairs,' recorded the unit war diary. The same was true of its pilot, and he spent four months in hospitals at Valenciennes, Bochum, and Münich. The legend would have it that he was ordered to report to Boblingen to convalesce, but returned directly to the front, claiming he could not find the town on the map. Be that as it may, the more prosaic personnel records show him being posted as a fighter pilot in mid-February 1917 to Bruno Lörzer's 26th Fighter Squadron in the Upper Alsace.
>
> Ten days later, Goering signed this combat report: 'Took off (in Albatros 3, D 2049) March 16, 1917, with 1st Lt Lörzer on pursuit mission. At about 4.30 PM, I saw three Nieuports attacking two German biplanes. I immediately closed on the nearest hostile, and loosed off a few short bursts at it. I then attacked the second Nieuport, which suddenly lost height, and made off at a low altitude.'
>
> On April 23rd, the record shows, he shot a British biplane out of a flight of four, and saw it go down in flames northeast of Arras. Five days later, he reported a dogfight with six Sopwiths over St Quentin: he expended 370 rounds of ammunition, and had the satisfaction of seeing one Englishman spinning out of control into the German lines.
>
> On April 28, 1917, Goering reportedly shot down a Sopwith aircraft.

> On the 29th, Goering shot down a Nieuport, watched it crash, and learned later that the British pilot, a Flight Lt Fletcher, survived with a bullet in his leg. 'As I flew on to Bohain at 300 feet,' he reported that night, 'a second enemy single-seat swooped down, pursued by an Albatros. The Englishman briefly attacked me, and shot out my rudder ... I could not see what happened then, as I had my hands full flying my plane without a rudder.'
>
> These dry reports give something of the flavor of air combat in those days. On May 17th, he had been given command of 27th Fighter Squadron, operating from the same field as Lörzer at Iseghem near Ypres.

Of this same period, Manvell and Fraenkel write, beginning with the November 1916 crash landing:

> He was operated upon for a serious wound in the hip from which he might easily have bled to death had expert care not been immediately available. Goering was immobilized for the greater part of a year. While he was convalescing, he had his first recorded love affair, with a girl named Marianne Mauser, the beautiful daughter of a well-to-do farmer near Mauterndorf.
>
> Her parents were undistinguished, but even so they did not permit the young couple to reach the point of an engagement. Herr Mauser regarded the matter shrewdly: a flier might be a romantic figure, but his expectation of life, unfortunately, was short.

Command of the 27th Fighter Squadron

Goering's main post-First World War Nazi biographer was Dr Erich Gritzbach, who noted in *Hermann Goering: The Man and His Work*:

> In May 1917, Goering was placed in charge of the 27th Squadron. His duty henceforth was not merely to be a pattern of daring and courage to his comrades as in the past—he had now to take charge of his squadron, and to lead younger and older soldiers to victory. As in the past, he was still utterly indifferent with regard to his own fate, while as captain of his squadron, he showed himself extremely anxious about the risks run by his men.
>
> The German Air Force had its unwritten laws. No quarter was given while a fight was going on, but when an enemy was put out of action, the German airman always treated his beaten foes with truly knightly consideration.

The following incident—described by a Dane, Capt. Paulli Krause-Jensen, who fought in the First World War on the side of France against Germany—testifies to the esteem in which Goering was held by his enemies.

> My encounter with the last commander of the dreaded Richthofen Squadron, the present Gen. Goering, was an unforgettable experience. We all knew, of course, the machines of our most outstanding opponents, and as a result of long-continued observation, we were to a certain extent familiar with their tactics in battle.

> I was one day alone on an extensive scouting trip with my machine, and I had taken some photographs when, in the distance, I was able to discern a German airplane returning from the French front. As we were bound to meet, I felt an overwhelmingly curiosity to make out who this lone flier might be.
>
> My opponent had also seen me, and was making in my direction. We both reconnoitered for a while, and cruised around one another in wide circles. For my part, I was not at all keen on getting into conflict with him just then, as I was anxious to get home, but he suddenly gave battle, and I had of course to reply. We kept flying round one another in ever narrowing circles, without succeeding in doing any damage to one another, and then suddenly the German machine swerved at a very sharp tangent, looped the loop, and in a moment had its machine gun trained on me.
>
> It all happened so suddenly that I was utterly unable to retort effectively. I immediately decided that I was encountering a very skilful opponent, and just then my enemy's plane cut another of those capers that were almost impossible feats in those days, and I knew at once that I was dealing with Capt. Goering, the squadron commander.
>
> Every great airman has his own special tactics. That kind of flying, however, I knew, was a trick of Goering's that no other airman could manage.
>
> I put up such a fight against him as I had never before put up. I flew better than I ever flew in my life, as I had my machine in perfect control, but I knew in my heart that I was facing a foe who was more competent than myself. It was no mere cat-and-mouse game, but it was impossible for me to beat such a brilliant airman as Goering. I don't know how long we continued circling around one another. Shreds of linen hanging from the wings of my machine showed that he had hit it many times, but he had so far failed to give me the knockout blow.
>
> Unfortunately, just as I had managed to get into a very favourable strategic position, my machine gun failed. I hammered with my bare fists against the red-hot weapon, but all to no avail. I tugged at the belt, but in vain. I stoically decided that it was all up with me.
>
> My opponent, however, evidently was surprised to see that I no longer fired at him. He kept circling around me, and seeing me hammering helplessly at my machine gun, realized at once that I was unable to fight any longer, and then suddenly—and this was the greatest moment in my entire experience as an airman—he flew quite close to me—his hand came to his cap with the military salute.
>
> Then, wheeling round, he flew off towards the German lines. Since that moment, I have always held the Germans in honor!

Postwar Allied biographers of Goering seem inclined to pooh-pooh this hagiographic account of the noble flier Goering, but I present it here nonetheless.

Another subject for differing accounts is that of his enforced hospitalization following his shooting down. Manvell and Fraenkel state:

> Goering was immobilized for the greater part of a year. While he was convalescing … the new concept of the 'air ace' was being created on the battlefronts. The fighter pilot who faced death in a deadly duel of wits with men as skilled in endurance as himself, and who flew high above the mud and degradation of earthbound warfare, became a new hero whose photograph stole the publicity.

The names of Richthofen and Udet became admired alike by the Germans and the Allies, because their exploits or those of their comrades became exciting news. Lörzer was appointed commander of Field Squadron 26, based at Mulhouse, where Goering joined him again on his discharge from hospital in 1916.

In Aachen one bright day, Lörzer saved Goering's life when he was being set upon by three French fighters; once more he only just made the ground with a machine punctured by bullets, its undercarriage in fragments, but Goering had done the same for Lörzer on a previous occasion. This was the quick-witted war of the air, with its own comradeship based on a mutual trust in skill.

Reportedly, Goering's third kill—a twin-engine French Caudron airplane—was made on 30 July 1916. Mosley writes:

Goering reported back for duty on November 3, 1916, on the day that Oswald Boelcke—shot down two days before—was given a great funeral with full military honours ... Goering was now attached to *Jagdstaffel 26*, of which Bruno Lörzer had been made commander, and their squadron—stationed at Mühlhausen—was too far away to be concerned with the ceremonials, but Lörzer had decided that Boelcke's burial should be commemorated by the destruction of some enemy planes, and Goering found himself in the air—and on the hunt—within hours of his arrival.

The squadron failed to find an enemy that day, but in subsequent weeks they more than made up for the lack.

As a fighter pilot, Goering ... had skill and guts, and it would never be said of him that he failed to accept a chance, or fled from an enemy. By mid–1917, he had shot down 17 planes, earned two more medals to go with his Iron Cross, and so won his spurs that he was made commander of a new squadron, *Jagdstaffel 27*, that flew with Lörzer's unit out of Iseghem, on the Flanders front [as we saw earlier].

The air war was hotting up, and the British and French—now equipped with new planes and synchronized guns, and some daredevil new pilots from the United States—had equalized the odds in the air, even if they had not yet wrested back the mastery of it.

Though they now operated two separate squadrons, the bond between Lörzer and Goering had grown stronger. In the dogfights over Flanders, each had intervened on the other's behalf during critical moments in the battle, and saved his friend from destruction. Goering had one lucky escape when Lörzer drove off three French fighters and allowed him to crash land, his craft riddled with bullets, but himself unharmed, and Goering once had jumped a British pilot who was just about to hit Lörzer's plane from the blind side.

'We are bound together by something stronger than chains, Lörzer and I,' Goering wrote to his sister. 'I know that in my hour of need, he will never let me down.'

Willi Frischauer notes:

The British Royal Flying Corps in those days had a great reputation, but the German enemy offered a spirited resistance. Mercilessly, the British air forces pounded the German infantry. As the German *Jastas* were getting into their stride, they met even larger British formations. Few aerodromes were safe from their attack.

The battle swayed back and forth, and *Jasta 26* was constantly on the move. By the spring of 1917, the big British offensive in Flanders was getting underway when Goering received his appointment as commander of *Jasta 27*. He had caught up with Lörzer again. The two *Jastas* shared the aerodrome near Iseghem near Ypres, and were in daily combat with the combined Anglo-French air forces.

Both sides fought cleanly. Chivalry and personal respect for a brave opponent were matters of course in both camps. Though there were great improvements in the types of aircraft employed, it was still chiefly a fight of man-against-man, with pilots pulling the trigger only when they were able to see the white of their enemy's eye.

Lt Goering quickly distinguished himself in these battles. He was now a crack airman. ... The details of one encounter, at least, remained deeply ingrained in Hermann Goering's memory. It started very much like any other dogfight in the air. Goering's opponent was an Englishman, a fine airman who—in the middle of an involved air battle—had deliberately sought out the leader of the German formation.

Turning and looping, diving, and again climbing, the two combatants strained every nerve to get each other in their sights. Away from their formations, they cut through the sky, twisting to get an advantage over the other. It was like a battle of life and death. Those who watched from the ground knew that the engagement would not be broken off without a decision.

After an exhausting 10 minutes, the decision went to Goering, but almost miraculously, the English pilot—his aircraft shot to ribbons—managed to glide off on a steep dive, and to land behind the German lines.

A few minutes later, Goering was by his side: 'My name is Hermann Goering!' said the victorious German. 'I think he said that his name was Slee,' Goering mused, as he told the story at the German Airmen's Club in Berlin 20 years later. 'He was a famous English pilot who had brought down a number of our comrades.' They shook hands and congratulated each other on their skill. Goering's narrow escape in this battle left him with a healthy respect for the British Royal Flying Corps.

Manvell and Fraenkel add:

By 1917, Goering's reputation as a fighter pilot was fully established. In addition to the Iron Cross, he was to be awarded the Zahringer Lion with Swords, the Karl Friedrich Order, and the Hohenzollern Medal with Swords, Third Class, all prior to his final award, the *Pour le Mérite*.

In May, he was put in command of Squadron 27, which needed an improvement in morale. Goering was now responsible for both administration and strategy; he had to show inspiring leadership. He set about the immediate strengthening of the squadron, working day and night to ensure efficiency, first on the ground and then in the air. In the summer the two squadrons—26 and 27—were operating alongside each other, flying from the same airdrome on the Flanders Front—at Iseghem, near Ypres.

The air attacks on the Allies were now built up into a major offensive. Goering's squadron in particular had to help in the protection of the other planes, attracting enemy fire away from them. The Allies, meanwhile, were redoubling their efforts in the air, and the Germans countered by forming especially large composite squadrons, called *Jagdgeschwader* (Pursuit Squadrons), equaling four of the others; the first of these was commanded by Manfred von Richthofen.

Goering and Lörzer were among those whose squadrons were merged to create the third of these major formations.

Goering versus Beaumont

Butler and Young write:

One British officer has good reason to remember Lt Goering at this time. Capt. Frank Beaumont, a pilot of No. 56 Squadron, Royal Flying Corps, that had fought many bitter battles with Goering's fliers, was extremely irritated when one day, after he had shot down two German aircraft, the wing of his own machine—for some reason which he could not understand—disintegrated. He was, nevertheless, able to bring his machine down behind the German lines with no more injury to himself than a slightly damaged foot, and was delighted to find the first days of his imprisonment alleviated by several visits from a Lt Goering, who brought him cigarettes, chocolate, and other comforts, spoke with warm admiration of 56 Squadron and, without ever trying to draw military information from him, contrived to have several pleasant conversations on matters of interest to airmen on both sides of the front—conversations that he always kept on extremely general lines.

'For God's sake,' Goering said to the young officer, 'don't get into the Army's hands! Stay with us if you possibly can. We'll look after you, and you'll have a much better time.' Capt. Beaumont, however, was not master of his own fate, and soon he was taken away to a prisoner-of-war camp, and for the present saw the kindly young German officer no more.

Now a full lieutenant, Goering meanwhile succeeded in overcoming the scruples of the Mauser family, and in the autumn of 1917, he and Marianne were officially betrothed.

Goering versus Slee

Of this same period, Gritzbach writes:

June 8, 1917, the unnatural heat of an early summer brooded with an enervating depression over the shell-torn country. The commander of the 27th Squadron was the first that morning on the airfield. At six o'clock sharp, he was studying the weather outlook. The sun was shining brightly in the sky. He decided to take advantage of the relative coolness of that early hour: 20 minutes later, the whole squadron was flying in close formation under his leadership in a northwesterly direction.

It was under orders to fly to the support of the 4th Army in Flanders. The battle had flared up in the Wytschaete sector. The big English offensive in Flanders that was to drag out into the winter had just started. Flooded with sunshine, Lille lay in front of the squadron. The visibility was excellent except towards the south in the direction of Arras, where a dense fog hung. It gave a wonderfully thrilling feeling to Goering to fly in the glorious morning sunshine, while his mind was awhirl with expectation of what the next few hours might bring to him.

Behind his plane came in squadron formation the machines of his young followers. Goering had only been in charge of them for a short time, and he had not so far sufficiently tested their skill as pilots, and for this reason, he was very much on the alert to prevent the enemy from attacking one of them in the rear and bringing him down before he would come to his aid. All his men were very young and inexperienced in the maneuvering of chaser planes.

The squadron was about 12,000 feet up in the air, when it flew over the Lys and reached the fighting zone. Beneath it, a fierce battle was raging all along the whole front.

The earth was being churned up with drumfire and mines, but Goering had no time to spare for watching the battle that was being waged beneath. He had to scout for his enemies in the air and beat them, and he did not have to wait for very long. Right above his squadron there suddenly appeared a Nieuport squadron of 16 units. It was difficult to recognize the little silver-grey fighters. They came along swiftly through the sunlit sky and swooped down on the last units of the squadron. The attack had begun.

Goering's squadron had spread too quickly, and it was not now in a position to fight a concerted battle, but Goering kept a lynx eye on his young followers. Whenever any of them was in danger, he charged in with a view to giving him a chance to get away. Now he attacked one enemy plane, now another, in order to support those who were in distress, but all his young pilots fought bravely, and hurried the enemy back behind their own lines.

During the course of the fighting, Goering's squadron had come down lower and lower. He was just having a breathing space after the wild turmoil of the fight, when he suddenly saw over his head an enemy who had swooped along stealthily from the direction of the sun in the hope of pouncing on the leader above and from the rear. Goering was familiar with the trick, and lured him on. The Englishman had tactically the better position, while Goering had a better machine and a more favorable wind—and so the duel started.

The enemy now believed that he had hit on the right moment, and swooped down like a hawk on the German machine. Now that was what Goering expected. He dived speedily in order to be able to move with more force, and then wheeling round with the speed of lightning, he darted upwards towards his opponent, at the same time opening fire with two machine guns.

Instead of tackling him from behind by surprise, Goering went straight ahead for the Englishman, and so the attacker was now the attacked. Goering's shots told, and his opponent swerved immediately in order to get away. Goering forthwith pounced on him and drove him farther and farther down with his fire. A wild, zigzag chase began. They wheeled to the right and the left, they looped the loop, turned, shot upwards, and almost immediately afterwards nose-dived.

They both tried all possible tricks and dodges, in their efforts to attack one another in the rear, to out-climb one another, and to force one another into the inner circle in order to take a better aim. They frequently darted past one another at such a sharp angle that the people on the ground thought that they had come into collision.

> The Englishman flew gracefully and skilfully. Goering could see him plainly seated in his machine. It was a stubborn fight in which neither would give way, as each was hopeful of victory. Then suddenly, Goering dived, and his enemy—seeing his chance—fired with both guns at him, hitting him several times, but Goering soared upwards again, and fired in his turn on the Englishman, apparently with telling effect, too.
>
> He nose-dived past Goering and made an effort to get away ahead of him, but Goering was instantly in hot pursuit of him. The Englishman tried the effect of zigzag movements in order to get out of the range of fire. By this time, they were both only 6,000 feet above the ground. Once more, the Englishman assumed the offensive. Goering had only a few cartridges left, and he was determined to be as economical as possible in using them.
>
> He was also determined to finish the job as quickly as possible, as he was already beginning to feel sick from the effects of the dizzy whirling about in the air, but the Englishman put up a desperate fight. Goering saw that there was nothing for it but to make a last desperate bid, and so from very close range, he aimed a well-directed burst of machine gun fire at the Englishman, who immediately turned topsy-turvy and nose-dived.
>
> Luckily, however, he was thrown out of it unhurt. By this time, Goering's strength, too, was utterly exhausted. His knees trembled, his pulse beat feverishly, and he was all bathed in perspiration as he flew to the nearest aerodrome. A telephone message came along the front that his opponent had been taken prisoner. He was an experienced fighter scout who had shot down five German planes.
>
> A few hours later, Goering had an opportunity of chatting with him. After the manner of airmen, they exchanged compliments about the hard fight they had put up, but when Goering wrote home, he said, 'Well, it is better after all that Mr Slee should be No. 8 on my list of victories than that I should be No. 6 on his list!'

Two days later—according to Irving:

> [...] on 8 June 1917: Attack a Nieuport [stated a Goering after-action report] that engaged me from above. I gave chase. In a protracted duel, he kept recovering and attacking me. Finally, I forced him down at Moorstedt, where he flipped over and caught fire. The dogfight had been watched by the entire eight fighter squadrons, either from the ground or from the air, so there can be no question of any other plane claiming this one; 500 rounds expended.

This victory was credited to him, but not others. On 7 July, he engaged a Spad, lost sight of it as hot oil was sprayed into his face, then believed he saw it crashing west of Ypres; but he was denied the credit. Nine days later, he attacked a patrol of Sopwith single-seats and shot one down on the second pass: 'Immediately after that, I had to take on a second hostile, that I forced down to about 600 feet, but my engine had caught some bullets and suddenly began to race.'

It just spun in its mounting, and my plane at once went into a spin. I put the plane down behind our third line of trenches and flipped over. The second hostile, therefore, got clean away. Goering.

He was allowed the next claim, a Martinsyde destroyed south of Passchendaele on the 24th. That was No. 10. On August 5th, he downed his 11th, another Sopwith:

> At 8.15 PM, I attacked an enemy force of nine single-seats with my squadron. They were fast biplanes. I dived on the leading hostile ... closed right in to about 150 feet, and opened fire. Suddenly, flames and thick smoke belched out of the plane, and the hostile spiralled down into dense cloud.
>
> I plunged in after him, but could not find him beneath the clouds, as there was a lot of haze at the lower levels. I had clearly seen the plane on fire. Fired 260 rounds. Goering.

It pained Goering that his slim-waist aviator's uniform still lacked the highest Prussian decoration—the blue enamel cross of the *Pour le Mérite*, the 'Blue Max'—but as a fighter ace, he was still way down the 'league table'.

On 1 November 1917, the top air ace was the Red Baron, Manfred von Richthofen, with 61 kills ... Goering and Lörzer had scored 15 each, and their friend Ernst Udet one fewer; 30 years later, Lörzer would snicker to fellow generals that his buddy Lt Goering had inflated his mission claims. 'Do the same,' Lörzer claimed Goering had urged him, 'otherwise, we'll never get ahead!'

Despite his robust good looks, his general health caused more problems than his war injuries. In February 1918, he was hospitalized with a throat infection for several weeks. In his absence, the Germans began stitching their fighter units into larger formations, using four squadrons in a *Geschwader* [Wing].

Goering's own bylined aerial combat article, July 1933

In the July 1933 edition of the British magazine *Popular Flying*, as 'Hauptmann Hermann Goering' he published an article entitled 'My Most Thrilling Combat: A Gallant British Airman':

> Looking back over four years of war experiences—when every day brought its quota of adventure and thrills—it may be a little difficult to decide exactly which experience has made the deepest impression on one's memory.
>
> But in my own case, it was certainly the fight with a famous English pilot that I like to call my '17th victory' that taught me what sensation really means. This is the story: In February 1918, I was leading out four planes of my *staffel* towards the front when—in spite of the fact that we were still well inside the German front lines—we were attacked by two English fighter airplanes that I had already observed flying above us.
>
> By the markings on his wings, I immediately spotted the leader, and without more ado, he and I closed in battle—and what a battle it was! First up, then down—at one moment, we were at a height of 4,500 metres; the next, we'd fallen to 2,000 only to climb again to 3,000.
>
> Without ceasing a moment, our machine guns blazed at each other, and I was very soon conscious of the fact that my plane was riddled with holes. Providence or miracle it must have

been that saved me from getting wounded. Never in all my four years' experience as a fighting aviator had I met with such an adversary! Never had I met such stubbornness and tenacity.

In the space of that few minutes' fighting, we went through all the possible experiences of flying—we spiralled, we looped, we side-slipped—and always we stuck together, neither of us leaving the other for a moment's respite.

I was, however, fast losing power, and knew that the battle could not last much longer, as far as I was concerned. Then—at a height of about 1,000 metres—by making an unexpected right-about turn, I managed to come round on the tail of my opponent, and give him full fire at close range.

This manoeuvre won me the fight. He fell, his engine giving full out, as he plunged headlong to Earth. They found the machine a mass of wreckage close behind the German lines, and the pilot—when they had extricated him from the debris—was discovered to have three shots through the head, and no fewer than seven through the chest.

He had put up a gallant fight, and we buried him with full military honours.

From the papers that were found on his body, we learned that my brave adversary was no less a person than the famous Capt. Craig, known all along the line for his audacity and daring, and whose squadron was never complete by the reason of the terrible losses that it always sustained.

The two machines that had attacked us—the second of which was also brought down in the same fight—turned out to be the last survivors of that famous squadron. For my own part, on coming down and looking over my machine, I discovered that my fuselage, rudder, and gravity tank were literally riddled with bullets.

An editor's boxed note at the end of Goering's piece states:

This space was kept open for particulars of Capt. Craig, about whom we have approached the Air Ministry. Up to the time of going to press, no information has been received, so we are unable to say anything about the very gallant officer who gave Capt. Goering such a hard fight. Perhaps a reader can help us?

The Pour le Mérite awarded at last, 2 June 1918

Irving continues:

Von Richthofen was given Wing No. 1, and Lörzer No. 2. Goering was consumed by an envy that was only partly allayed by the Kaiser's award, at last, of the *Pour le Mérite* on June 2, 1918. Richthofen had been shot down and killed on April 21, 1918, but Goering was passed over as his successor. He now had 18 official kills.

On June 5th, he gunned down a biplane near Villers and four days later—flying a Fokker distinguished by a white engine cowling and white tail—he poured 200 rounds into a Spad prowling at low level along the front lines. 'He plunged vertically like a rock from 1,300 feet, and impacted at the northwestern corner of the horseshoe wood south of Coroy behind our front lines.'

Blood-Ryan gives this account of how Goering learned of his being awarded the 'Blue Max':

> May 1918, somewhere in France. Goering is about to start off on a flight over enemy lines. His adjutant detains him ... 'Lt Goering! ... A report has just come in from GHQ that the Emperor has bestowed upon you the Order *Pour le Mérite*!'
>
> 'That's no reason for you to burst your lungs shouting at me, is it?' grins Goering with satisfaction, and with that he taxies across the field to new fights and new victories.

Twentieth victory achieved—and the Red Baron's first successor

'I circled several times over the crash site.' Kill No. 20 was a Spad that Goering shot down on 9 June 1918. On the 17th he destroyed another Spad near Ambleny.

Goering led a memorial service for von Richthofen on 24 April 1918, according to Mosley:

> That same afternoon, his squadron was back in business, and Goering had the satisfaction of shooting down a Sopwith of the same type that had destroyed his own pilots as well as the Red Knight ... To the surprise of everyone in the 'Flying Circus', von Richthofen had named Capt. Wilhelm Reinhard as his successor as commander of *JG 1*.
>
> Reinhard was the oldest man in the super unit at 27, but that was not the reason for his fellow pilots' stupefaction. It was, in fact, his generally recognized maturity of judgment that had probably influenced von Richthofen in naming him, but though he had solidity, courage, and great professionalism, he lacked one quality that the 'Flying Circus' needed if it was to go on being the formidable scourge of the Allied air arm over Flanders. He had no flexibility.
>
> He was strictly a textbook flier who went entirely by the rules, and anyone who operated accordingly over the battlefield these days was unlikely to achieve any of the spectacular successes that Germany was now demanding of its fliers.
>
> It did not help Reinhard's leadership that he recognized his own weakness, and almost always when battle was joined with the enemy, immediately delegated the tactics for the dogfight to one or other of the pilots under him. He wrote in his daybook after one of his men had been shot down in battle, 'He had the makings of an outstanding leader, and in the air, I yielded to his guidance.'
>
> It was only thanks to this modest delegation of authority that the 'Flying Circus' (it had now been officially dubbed *JG Richthofen 1*) had some notable successes during the first weeks of May, and on the 15th of that month, it shot no fewer than 13 British bombers and fighters out of the sky. On May 20th, the super squadron received orders to leave its headquarters at Cappy and fly into Guise, in preparation for a great offensive that Gen. Erich Ludendorff was mounting against Allied armies on the River Aisne.
>
> The pilots were glad to go, because Cappy had too many memories associated with it of the master ace and his scarlet coloured plane. On arrival at Guise, they were informed that they and several other squadrons on the front were to be re-equipped with an entirely new plane in preparation for the forthcoming offensive. This was the Fokker D.VII biplane that was to replace the Fokker triplane that they had been flying up to now.

The pilots received the news with anything but pleasure, for rumour had preceded the new machine, and had it that the biplane was sloppy in performance, and lacked the speed of climb and tightness of manoeuvre that had typified the triplane.

They flew it, however, for the next few weeks without any notable disasters, but much was their relief when they heard that yet another new plane would shortly be coming off the production lines, and that this one was a superbly capable warplane.

It was the Fokker D.VIII, a monoplane that the British and Americans later christened the Flying Razor. On July 3, 1918, a number of squadron commanders on the Western Front were summoned to Adlershof to test the new plane, and among them were Hermann Goering and the new 'Flying Circus' commander, Wilhelm Reinhard.

Both men put the plane through its paces, and afterwards expressed themselves more than well satisfied with its performance. They then retired to the mess to talk and drink with young Anthony Fokker.

When they came out again, Goering's eye was caught by a peculiar-looking biplane that was parked to one side of the airfield, and when he asked about it, he was told that it was an experimental craft designed by Dr Claudius Dornier (who was later to build a fleet of famous flying boats), and that it had been constructed by the Zeppelin Company.

Goering said he would like to try it out, and after some hesitation, he was given a quick explanation of the controls, the plane was fuelled up, and he taxied it out onto the grass and took off. Finding the Dornier extraordinarily mobile and manoeuvrable, he then proceeded to give a spectacular exhibition of aerobatics. To use an old fighter pilot's term, he 'beat up' the airfield at practically nought feet, both right side up and upside down.

He looped and spinned and yawed, and, finally—after a particularly awe-inspiring flight down the airfield on canted wings, he brought it to a landing and leaped out, laughing with delight at the expressions on the faces of the spectators.

Not to be outdone, Wilhelm Reinhard declared that he would now show what could be done with the awkward-looking plane. He waited for it to be refuelled, and then took off and almost immediately went into a steep climb from which he showed no signs of levelling off, even when he had reached more than 3,000 feet.

Suddenly, there was a report like a pistol shot, and the watchers below were horrified to see the plane's portside wing crumple and then break away. The Dornier went into a spin and crashed headlong into the earth. When they reached the wreckage, they saw that a wing strut had broken under pressure. The commander of *JG Richthofen 1* was dead.

Capt. Reinhard's successor, 7 July 1918

Mosley continues:

> Who would succeed him as commander of what was by now the world's most famous group of combat fliers? There were two favourites among the pilots of *JG Richthofen 1*. One was Ernst Udet, and the other Carl Löwenhardt, and they were bitter rivals, not only for Richthofen's command but also in the race to beat the master ace's record of 80 kills.

On July 4, 1918, it was announced that Udet was being temporarily given control of the super squadron, but the following day, the order was withdrawn. Udet was certain he had lost the command because of Löwenhardt's intrigues, and there were rumours that he had gone so far as to challenge his rival to a sky duel.

Everyone waited for Löwenhardt's name to be announced as Udet's replacement, but instead—on the morning of July 7, 1918, the *JG* adjutant—Capt. Karl Bodenschatz—walked into the mess with a paper in his hand, and pompously announced that he was calling an immediate meeting of all pilots and mechanics in the main hangar. There he read them the notice that he had just received from Berlin.

'By direction of the Supreme Commander of the German Armed Forces,' he read, 'Lt Hermann Wilhelm Goering, *Pour le Mérite* … presently commanding *Jasta 27*, is hereby appointed commander of *JG Freiherr von Richthofen 1*.'

The crowd of pilots and men looked at each other in a heavy silence.

In *Goering: Air Leader*, Asher Lee adds:

His period of command of the Richthofen *Geschwader*—from July-November 1918—was one of disaster and retreat for which Goering was, of course, in no sense to blame. The French twin-engine Caudron bombers were proving difficult to shoot down because German fighter aircraft ammunition did not easily penetrate their armour plating.

The new British Sopwith Camel and SE.5 fighters and the French Spad 140 and 200 machines were technically superior to the Albatros plane with which the Richthofen *Geschwader* was now being fitted. The growing preponderance of Anglo-French air power ruled the skies on the Western Front, and made great holes in the ranks of Goering's fighter squadrons.

It is surprising to find that—less than a month after he was appointed to command the Richthofen Circus—Goering went off on four weeks' leave despite the state of German air crisis. Was this a habit of his? He certainly pursued it when he became commander-in-chief of the German Air Force in the late 1930s, and in the early 1940s.

When on leave, he took the opportunity of developing his contacts with the Fokker Aircraft industry and the German BMW Aeroengine Works.

Goering was generally interested in the technical problems of engines and equipment; he also had a keen business sense that was later to extend from aeronautics to economics, and the world of art.

Fokker was to help him with a fresh career when the crash of Germany's defeat came, and it was not long delayed.

The final phase and last victory

Butler and Young add:

The unit lost no time in resuming its business. On July 15, 1918, the War Diary read as follows: 'Attack by 7th Army. *Geschwader* engaged large numbers of enemy aircraft in the

Marne Valley. Morning, moderate flying activity. Afternoon, considerable enemy activity at all heights.

'Strong formations of English single-seat fighters particularly active. Individual groups of these squadrons concentrated into half-groups.'

The German retreat from the Marne had begun, and the enemy activity that had been recorded in the War Diary continued to increase. On July 18th, Goering shot down his 22nd [and last] enemy aircraft, and the *Geschwader*'s total bag was nine French and two British machines, but the greatly improved quality and equipment of the Allied machines was a constant worry.

As Goering himself wrote at the time, 'The enemy biplanes are very well armed, and fly in exceedingly good formation, even when attacked by a number of German fighters. They are equipped with armored or fireproof tanks.'

By August, the Germans were in full retreat, hotly pursued by the armies of the Allies. It became increasingly difficult to replace the German aircraft lost, harder still to find the successors of the skilled men who had died in them.

Anti-aircraft guns for the defence of aerodromes were at a premium. Day after day, the Richthofen *Geschwader* lost one or two of its best airmen, and sometimes Goering—looking down its nominal rolls—observed with consternation that his command was no more than half-strength.

Nevertheless, the *Geschwader*'s total score of enemy aircraft destroyed since its formation, some nine months before, was 500.

Goering versus Sholto-Douglas

Frischauer writes:

The Richthofen Circus—as it was called by friend and foe—was moved up and down the line to intervene wherever the weakening front showed signs of breaking. Reeling back the German forces, the British 5th Army was on the offensive, supported by the crack No. 84 Fighter Squadron, equipped with the SE.5As, the best fighter aircraft of the day.

Commanding Squadron 84 was Capt. William Sholto-Douglas, one of Britain's outstanding young airmen. Wherever the Richthofen Circus appeared, Squadron 84 was there to match its strength with that of the Germans … 'We knew Goering's aircraft,' Lord Douglas told me when we discussed the fateful battles of his youth. The German planes were painted in bright colours—the British thought it was done to terrify them, but the practice was actually adapted for the purpose of easy recognition.

'I have once or twice "revved around" in a dogfight with a purple and yellow German aircraft that I took to be Goering's,' Lord Douglas said, 'but as we were both at this time highly experienced fighter pilots, we never succeeded in getting our sights on each other.'

Reports from one of his squadron leaders sadly admitted that the British Sopwith aircraft were technically superior to the Albatros D … It was the same with the SE.5As and the Spad 140 Ps and 200 Ps, that both beat the Albatros in climbing power and manoeuvrability. Along the whole line, the British superiority in quality and numbers was telling.

> One after another of the air aces who had been the pillars of the Richthofen Squadron went over—never to return. 'There is little conversation in the mess,' noted Bodenschatz in his War Diary. Finally, the inevitable order arrived, signed by the Crown Prince: 'Owing to the great losses that the group has suffered, I order the reorganization of the group into a squadron. It is to co-operate with Group No. 3 under the command of Greim;' 26 years later, Hitler appointed Greim to succeed Hermann Goering as C-in-C of the Luftwaffe ...
>
> On September 1, 1918, Goering himself wrote a report about the situation: 'On the fronts of the 2nd and 7th Armies, enemy balloons have been attacked on several occasions without catching fire.'
>
> 'Actually, nothing can be done anymore,' Bodenschatz wrote. 'The features of Lt Goering are getting harder.' ... The spirits of the young commander dropped. He was hoping for the winter to stem the tide of enemy squadrons that were darkening the skies over him.
>
> By the end of October 1918, Goering's unit had dwindled to 63 officers and 484 other ranks, including administrative staff and cooks [a sizeable unit for a lieutenant to command, at any rate].

By now—in the autumn of 1918—there were rumors of revolution at home, followed by the double abdications of the Kaiser and German Crown Prince, as well as the heads of all the German royal and princely houses.

Frischauer continues:

> By November 9, 1918, it was obvious that the end had come. Goering made a heroic gesture. Bodenschatz told me how he called his officers together and asked them to be prepared for any eventuality, for a last death-and-glory battle. It was a vain gesture. Germany's fighting days were over. There were rumours that the Armistice that was to be signed would provide for their aircraft to be handed over to the Americans, but Goering—from a welter of orders and counter-orders—hurriedly chose an instruction to fly to Darmstadt.
>
> Ordering Bodenschatz to take the ground staff and the equipment by road, the commander and his men took off for the last time to fly towards the Fatherland. In Darmstadt, it appeared that some of the pilots had lost their way and landed in Mannheim, where a revolutionary 'Soldiers' Council' was already in control of the aerodrome. The airmen had been deprived of their arms.
>
> As soon as Goering received the news, he sent a peremptory message: 'Let my men join me with their weapons, or I'll come and bomb you all to bits!' The ultimatum was effective, and the stragglers were allowed to rejoin their unit [fully armed].
>
> The final battle came with an order to surrender their machines to the French in Strasbourg. 'I am afraid you will have to comply,' Goering told the air crews grimly, 'but make sure that the French shall not get what they expect!' The men understood his hint.
>
> The Richthofen Circus virtually crashed down on Strasbourg. Many of the planes were almost completely wrecked on landing. Goering always thought of the incident as a 'successful operation', his final act of defiance.

> Now he wrote his last official report: 'Since its inception, the squadron has gained 644 victories in the air. Losses inflicted by the enemy amounted to 56 officers and pilots, and six other ranks killed; 52 officers and seven other ranks wounded. Signed, Hermann Goering, lieutenant and *Geschwader* commander.'

Manvell and Fraenkel note that Goering was demobilized on 11 November 1918, with the honorary rank of *Hauptmann* in the old Bavarian town of Aschaffenburg. Butler and Young add:

> The *Geschwader* flew back to Aschaffenburg, where, on November 19, 1918, Goering took leave of his comrades in the *Stiftskeller* public house. He spoke to them of some of their unit's history, of its victories and losses, and of the strange time that lay ahead, an epoch in which they could already see all the values that they had cherished crashing to the ground, all of the old loyalties shattered.
>
> He spoke with feeling understandable in the circumstances, and many of those who listened wept a little. Then the speaker raised his glass.
>
> 'To the Richthofen *Geschwader*,' he cried, and they all drank. Goering drained his own glass, and—with a savage gesture—dashed it against the wall.
>
> Goering went through an experience familiar to those who still wore the uniform of an officer of the Imperial Army in the last days of 1918: he was set upon by a crowd of ex-soldiers, girls and women, hungry and haggard, whipped up by a Bolshevik agitator. They shouted, 'No more war!' and tried to tear the decorations from his tunic, as he thrust his way through the press.
>
> Only a few weeks before the incident, Goering had been one of Germany's heroes. Now the very decorations that testified to his service were a provocation to many of his countrymen.

Frischauer writes of this incident:

> Arriving in Münich in full uniform, he had to defend himself against one of these street attacks, and was only just able to save his decorations. He vowed that one day he would earn many more medals—and nobody ever was going to take them from him.

He would lose them all in 1945, however, when he was stripped of them by the Americans.

The current author experienced some of these same sentiments during 1965-67 over his own service in the US military, especially after returning home from the Vietnam War.

Goering ended the war as a captain, but would return to the air service in 1933, and, in March 1935, would create the second German Air Force, the later vaunted Luftwaffe.

Another take on Goering

Noted author Stephen Longstreet, in his 1970 work *The Canvas Falcons: The Men and Planes of World War I*, writes:

A number of men who were involved with the German flying efforts in World War I survived to become important figures in World War II's Luftwaffe: Udet, Fokker, and, of course, Hermann Wilhelm Goering (1893–1946).

The last was not then the sinister fat clown of that later conflict, but the slim, romantic, scheming ace of the earlier war, whose official record was 22 air victories. He was one of those silver spoon babies, who for as long as he could remember had been told that he was of a great family that could trace its fine blood ties back to royalty, to Hohenzollern and Wittelsbach ancestors ...

Those who earn a living by it have traced Goering's family line back to the 12th Century. The findings of the experts were always intended to show he was of 'pure Aryan stock' and descended from the line of Wolfgang von Goethe, from the Bismarcks, from the Count Zeppelins.

Because of Hohenzollern ties, Goering could claim kin to Wilhelm II ... as well as to Queen Victoria. Naturally, the Goerings were soldiers rather than poets, music makers, or painters ... There is no doubt that being left without a mother and father during those early years predisposed the boy to grow up a confused child, and a strange adult.

He always claimed he was Bavarian, as if the Marienbad Sanatorium was his homeland, the place of his birth. Six weeks after he was born, Mamma was gone. His actual caretaker was a Frau Graf, whom he called 'Mamma'. He grew into a pretty child, lonely, brooding over the mother, father, and older brothers and sisters he had never seen.

He began to invent fantasies early, bragged to other children. He was spoiled, overbearing, and cruel as only maladjusted children can be. Mrs Grau was an old widow, and had no place in her dry heart for this child left on her. Hermann got no affection, and he made no real friends with other children ...

The boy had a collection of toy soldiers ... painted in all the glory of uniforms of the past. These were his passion. He maintained a huge collection, even as an adult, and with the aid of a mirror, he imagined he had twice as many soldiers. The fantasy that was so much of his brutal nature, his selfishness, was actually a dream world in which he hid, to picture himself immortal and able to create miracles.

Hermann was a bad student. By the age of 12, five schools had tossed him out. By nature, he was vain, self-glorifying, had no respect for teachers. Uniforms—not chalk and books—were his dream, and he was delighted to be taken in by the Karlsruhe Academy. It was a school where the soldier-like stance, the rigid mind, orders, came first.

Here Hermann expanded, becoming the perfect soldier, the disciplined robot on parade. Here was the security of old soldiers, barked orders; order in everything. He was, on the surface, no longer insecure. Precision and direct punishment, a pat on the shoulder, a word of crisp praise for duty well done, replaced a lost mother.

He developed a veneer of German idealism, eager for Germany to seize its rightful place in the enemy world. This was a successful façade for the hurt, warped ego of a discarded child, but under the polished surface, he never felt at ease unless he was jesting, being funny, even witty.

For he had a good intellect, though totally lacking in true learning. Never a scholar, the sly, ingrown boy turned into the school charmer as a protective covering for his still sensitive fear of rejection. This—crossed with all those ancestors who had taken cities, chopped off heads, fought in Crusades, and died on the best horses to the smell of gunpowder—made for a complex youth.

Hermann ached for friendships; he now wanted to be liked, well liked ... When the war came, he cheerfully, hopefully, became a lieutenant in an infantry regiment where he served with no great glory in some early battles ...

Goering was passing himself off now as a trained observer. The two friends [Goering and Lörzer] flew together, and flew well, downing a French plane over Verdun. The other fliers called the strange pair 'The Odd Couple.' Goering took pilot's lessons and was soon flying two-seats for artillery spotting.

In 1916, Lörzer was in charge of *Jasta 26*, and Goering came over, now flying single-seat fighters, to become second in command. He was wounded in the thigh, but returned to head his own *Jasta*, the 27th. Goering was a good pilot, but not a great one. He was, however, an intelligent flier and made the most of what skill he had ...

He was getting plump; his figure was short and square, his stare blue-eyed and steady; the big jaw at this stage was still firm. Goering had four months of glory before the war ended. He was based at Tellencourt when the Armistice came, and the group was told to fly to Darmstadt to await orders.

The city was in the hands of a revolution, led by street fighters and soldiers, who stripped the first planes to land of their weapons. Goering roared that if the weapons were not returned to his fliers, he would call in the entire unit and bomb and machine gun the town. They got back their guns and took to the sky for Aschaffenburg.

Here, under Goering, the Richthofen Circus finally went out of business, disbanding its glory with the usual tears, body hugs, and swearing of eternal friendship, and oaths that the old Germany would rise again ...

There is no doubt that Goering's mind, in the shock of defeat, was already back in the fantasies of his childhood: revenge became paramount, and some high destiny awaited him.

'Hermann Goering, Amiable Psychopath'

Capt. Gilbert in his 1948 paper published in *The Journal of Abnormal and Social Psychology* writes:

> He had hardly graduated from Lichterfelde in 1913, when his father died. The following year—with the outbreak of World War I—he was committed to the front as a lieutenant in an infantry regiment. In discussing his war career, Goering glossed over his activities as an infantry officer, saying that he was more interested in aviation.
>
> No doubt it appealed more to his individualistic and recklessly demonstrative inclinations, but he also admitted suffering from claustrophobia in a tank, submarine, or Zeppelin gondola.
>
> He became a fighter pilot in 1916, was wounded and hospitalized for three months, then resumed his aviation career. He acquitted himself quite well as a pilot, running up a total of 28 planes shot down [*sic*] ...

> Aside from the glory which his reckless physical courage earned him, Goering had little to say about his activities as an officer ... At all events, during World War I, Goering made the dangerous and fateful discovery that war could bring both glory and profit to one who was sufficiently reckless, unscrupulous, and amiable.

Farewell to the Army, 1918

In Goering's farewell speech to his men in 1918, he said:

> The fight with weapons is over! In its stead rises—if we will—the new conflict of principles, of morals, of character! If we have lost our home, we will win it back once more. There was a time when our love for it was our strength, our glory, and our crown.
>
> Are we to look on inactive while this crown—for whose sake we strove night and day with death—is trodden in the dirt? Has our honour remained with those out there whose bodies are covered by the earth?
>
> No, unless we consent. No one will ever take from us our honour, our rights, and our freedom!

The Minister of War, Gen. Walter Reinhardt, ordered that when German officers appeared in uniform, they would wear no shoulder epaulettes, but instead blue sleeve stripes. In December 1918, a meeting was called to discuss the new order, and both the Minister and Goering were present at the Berlin Philharmonic Hall. Goering asserted:

> Mr Minister, I was convinced that you would be present here today, but I hoped to see a mourning band on your sleeve to express your deep regret for the wrong that you propose to do us. Instead, you are wearing the blue colours on your arm. Mr Minister, you should have chosen red! [Red was the color of the Communists.]
>
> We officers have done our duty for four long years on land, on sea, and in the air. We have risked life and limbs for our fatherland. Now, we have come home, and how are we treated? We are spat on; we are to be deprived of what was our honour. And—I tell you—it is not the people who are responsible.
>
> The people were our comrades—every one of them—whatever might be his rank, for the four years of the war. It is not the people—but those who have inflamed it—who stabbed our splendid army in the back and have no other wish but to rule, so that they may enrich themselves at the people's expense ...
>
> But the day will come—I know it, and I beg you to believe it—when these men will have shot their bolt, and when we shall kick them out, out of our Germany. Make yourselves ready—be prepared for that day—and work for it, for it will surely come!

Manvell and Fraenkel conclude, 'Goering left the hall, refusing to serve any longer in an Army that was ready to obey the degrading orders of a republican government.'

Above left: A slim, dapper, elegant, and handsome Lt Hermann Goering in white summer undress uniform and cigarette holder in the *Kasino* (Officers' Club) in German-occupied Metz, 1916.

Above right: Kilduff has captioned this photo 'In an early display of vanity, Goering commissioned an artist—Lt of Reserve Paul Birnstein—to paint his portrait after he was awarded the Iron Cross 1st Class. The work may not have been completed, as Birnstein was killed in a crash during pilot training at FEA 9 in Darmstadt on February 3, 1916.' Goering's own 1916 caption is much simpler: 'Birnstein works on my portrait.' Note the summer white uniform, a little different from the previous photo.

German air force hangar at Colmar, France, 1917. The future *JG 1* that Goering would command from July to November 1918 comprised four *Staffeln* (Squadrons).

Above and below: Twin wide-angle shots by lens man Goering of German hangars and planes. Goering's first flight as a fighter pilot over enemy lines was on 3 October 1915, with his observer manning a rear machine gun over Champagne in France versus seven French Air Force planes.

Goering's colleague pilot and ace Lt Kurt Wolff. Goering received his Pilot's Badge on 12 October 1915. He crashed on 1 December 1915 in a Gotha G.I bomber, during preparations for the 1916 Verdun offensive, and suffered a knee injury.

Above left: Lt Kurt Wolff (right) in discussion with an unknown man at left. Considered a daredevil by his fellow fliers, on 29 January 1916, Goering's plane was hit ten times by ground flak artillery.

Above right: A famous—and oft published—picture of Lt Kurt Wolff that I found in the Goering Albums. Did Goering himself take the photo? Note also the car at left. Like the fictional character Bruno Stachel in the novel *The Blue Max*, Goering often drove to crash sites to have his aerial victories confirmed.

Goering's caption is, 'Jagdstaffel/Jasta 26 at Colmar', February 1917, where Baron Manfred von Richthofen sits at top center with bandaged head and Lt Wolff below at center with left arm in sling. One contemporary asserted, 'And then there is Goering—a master pilot!'

Aviator Lt Ulrich Neckel (1898–1928), holder of the 'Blue Max', in another well-known photo from the Goering Albums, according to Bronnenkant. I disagree. In my view, this is, instead, Reserve Lt Hans Klein (1891–1944). He ended the Great War with twenty-two confirmed victories. Note the machine gun at center and the teddy bear mounted on the airplane wing above the rear-view mirror.

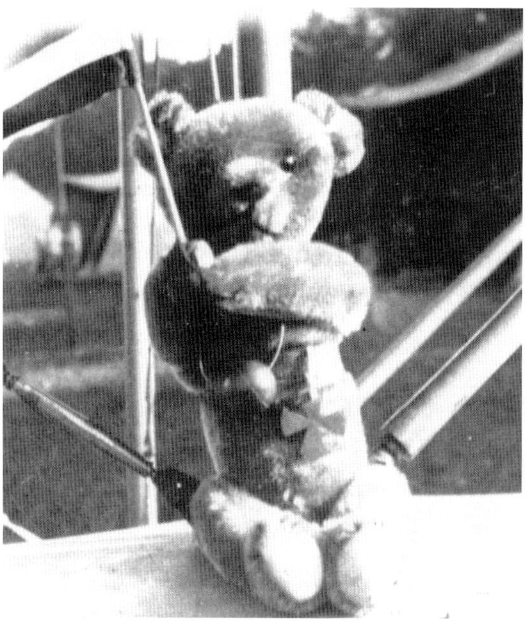

'The Teddy' is Goering's caption to this photo of another small plush toy mounted on an aircraft with a mock Iron Cross affixed to it. One Goering watcher called him, 'A Big Gun, a devil of a fellow!' His friend Bruno Lörzer was promoted to first lieutenant on 18 April 1916, ahead of Goering.

Fokker D.VIII Parasol monoplane, front view. The last of the Fokker fighter series, this October 1918 single-seat scout plane 'might have been the best in its line' according to one source. Coming online just two weeks before the Great War's end, it was called the Parasol Fokker by Ernst Udet, who flew it.

Fokker D.VIII Parasol monoplane, side view. It had a 140-hp Oberursel engine, a wingspan of 27 feet 3 inches, a speed of 125 mph, a ceiling of 21,000 feet, a length of 19 feet 5 inches, a weight of 1,331 pounds when fully loaded, and an endurance of 1½ hours. Its armament was a pair of fixed Spandau machine guns.

Above: German Gotha bomber. One admirer of Goering's aerial photography asserted, 'One sees every dugout and every detail.' On 9 July 1916, Goering was assigned to single-seat fighters.

Right: German Gotha bomber view, showing crew members at center and right. Another Goering admirer noted, 'He storms about vigorously!' over the French fortress of Metz.

Right side view of Goering's Halberstadt D.II fighter plane, as first published by me in 1998. On one day, Goering made 'nine flights and three aerial combats'. Later, 'he was making 11–14 flights daily'.

Kilduff has captioned this, 'Lt Hermann Goering in the cockpit of the Halberstadt D.II in which he fought off a patrol of British Nieuport fighters November 2, 1916.' Goering captions it simply, 'In my plane, with Kuhn, Capt. [Helmuth] Volkmann', 1915.

Halberstadt D.II aircraft, 1917. This was a 1916 single-seat fighter with either one or two fixed Spandau or Maxim machine guns. It was powered by a 120-hp Argus or Mercedes engine, with a wingspan of 28 feet 10 inches, a weight of 1,606 pounds when fully loaded, and a length of 23 feet 11 inches. Its speed was 90 mph at sea level, according to one source, and had a ceiling of 13,000 feet, with an endurance of 1½ hours.

German ace 1Lt Oswald Boelcke landed his new Roland C.III aircraft in 1916 in Montmédy, France; Goering's own photo. At first, Lörzer helped Goering into and out of his cockpit due to the latter's still painful arthritic rheumatism.

Seen here in left profile, Lt Oswald Boelcke prepares to deplane from his new Roland C.III, 1916.

Captioning this photo of the overall sequence, Kilduff writes, 'A photograph in Goering's album showed the top German fighter ace of the time, *Hauptmann* Oswald Boelcke, while test flying the LFG Roland C.II.' Boelcke died aged 25, as the result of a mid-air collision on 28 October 1916. With forty aerial victories, he was the twenty-seventh highest scoring fighter pilot of the war overall, and tenth among the Germans. Note especially the leather flight suit.

Rear view of Boelcke's unmanned Roland C.II plane. On 2 November 1916, Goering himself was shot down, and as a result was hospitalized for six weeks. Goering was named to command *Jasta 26* on 18 January 1917.

Right side view of Boelcke's unmanned Roland C.II aircraft, with two ground crewmen at left. On 2 November 1916, Goering suffered a painful hip wound. As *Staffelführer* of *Jasta 27*, he flew an Albatros fighter over Messines Ridge in Flanders on 7 June 1917, and also over Dunkirk, where, in 1940, his Luftwaffe famously failed to halt the sea-borne evacuation of the British Expeditionary Force in the Second World War.

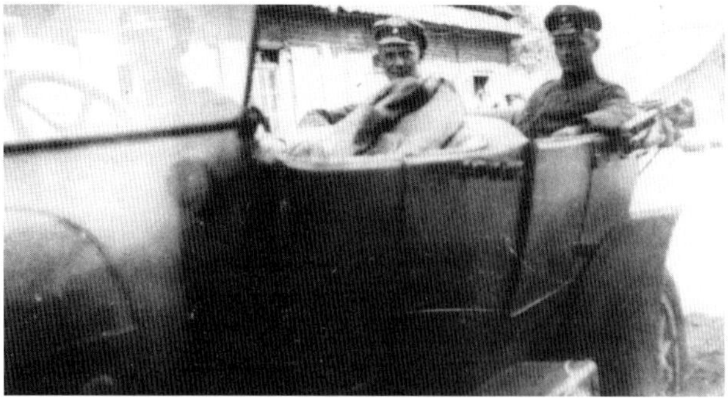

Variations on a theme: the first of four views of Lt Goering in period cars. This is most likely a Mercedes 12/32 PS from 1915–19; Goering sits in the back at the left. The other man and the driver are both unknown. The car had a four-cylinder, inline engine with a displacement of 3013 cc, and 32 hp at 1800 rpm. The chassis had a U-section pressed steel frame, with a wheelbase of 3075/3240 mm. It had a maximum speed of 70 kph, and a cable handbrake on the rear wheels.

As near as I can tell, Goering was the first, and thus also the earliest, of the future Nazi leaders to ride in a Mercedes car, as here, in this Mercedes-Knight 1910–13 open tourer, made under license from American Charles Knight. This photo was taken at Vouziers, France, during the First World War. Goering, smiling, sits immediately behind the driver on the left-hand side, in a mid-section jump seat. Note also that the license plate—V-1163—appears twice.

Kilduff has written of this third auto scene, 'Goering sat in the back seat of the car that brought his two French prisoners-of-war to be presented to General of Infantry Hans von Zwehl of the 5th Army Staff (left).'

The car serves only as a muted backdrop to the three men shown in this view. Kilduff has written, '1st Lt Hermann Goering (left) and Reserve Lt Willi Rosenstein (center) in happier times, discussing air operations with Lt Curt Rabe (right).'

'Hermann Goering marked the completion of his pilot's qualifications by posing in his training aeroplane at Freiburg,' Kilduff has noted. One Goering admirer wrote on 28 July 1917, 'I consider Lt Goering to be worthy of every decoration.'

Goering's caption reads, 'At the Brunelles airfield', 1915. Note also the Zeppelin hangar at the far left of the frame and the hangar behind the planes as well.

An Albatros C.III in transit. The C.III first entered service in 1916 as a two-seat reconnaissance, observation, and all-purpose aircraft. It had either a single 150-hp Benz or 160-hp Mercedes inline piston engine, a maximum speed of 87 mph, a climb to 3,280 feet in 9 minutes, and an endurance of 4 hours. Its wingspan was 38 feet 4¼ inches, it had a height of 10 feet, and a wing area of 397.31 square feet. Its armament consisted of a pair of 7.92-mm machine guns—one fixed and another trainable—and a small bomb load capacity.

A Fokker DR.I triplane at left and a trio of Albatros fighters at right. Goering was cited as having 'a very domineering personality and overly aggressive way of pressing for credit'.

A crashed Albatros C.III. Although—according to Lee—Goering was disliked, he nevertheless 'took part in every patrol'. He received the Hohenzollern House Order on 20 October 1917, a necessary prelude to being awarded the 'Blue Max'.

An Albatros C.III 'After being badly damaged in aerial combat. Goering's Albatros D.III 2049/16 carried him back to his airfield and then was finally scrapped. 'I've been flying for three years,' Goering noted. On 30 October 1917, he was involved in strafing Allied ground troops—a favorite tactic of Lörzer—as the Allies took Passchendaele in the Battle of Flanders in Belgium.

Above left: A third view of the same Goering Albatros. *Jasta 27* fought in both Belgium and Northern France starting on 1 November 1917. Goering was 'too stubborn and arrogant to admit he was wrong', a tendency noted by his own fighter and bomber pilots during the Second World War.

Above right: 'My sight-seeing visit in my GKFZ G.49,' is Goering's caption to this 1916 photo, which I first published in 1998. 'Now I feel a certain exhaustion,' Goering lamented, and joined *Jasta 26* on 15 February 1917. Suffering from 'life threatening' tonsillitis early in 1918, Goering was in Dreyse Field Hospital, where he was first administered morphine, to which he later became addicted.

Above left: Goering's 1917 caption reads, 'Me in my fighter, Albatros D.III 2049'. Kilduff has added '/16' after 2049; 'For a picture that eventually appeared on a popular Sanke postcard.' Asher Lee states, 'During the few months in which Goering commanded the Richthofen Fighter Group of *Jastas* under a single commander operating in Flanders' skies, it gained few fresh laurels in air combat. Pilot casualties were heavy … but no fault of leadership or courage can be reasonably ascribed to him personally.' Mosley notes, 'On the evening of July 17, 1918, Goering called all wing and *Jasta* leaders in once more, sketched out the operations which the *JG* would adopt on the following morning, and then dropped his bombshell. Each *Jasta* leader—instead of commanding his squadron as usual—would, on this operation, detach himself and hand over command to his second. All the *Jasta* leaders—including Udet, Loewenhardt, and Lothar von Richthofen—would come under Goering's personal command, and would fly with him.'

Above right: Goering's caption for this 1917 photo is 'Me in front of my machine'. Note the goggles on his cap. On 1 April 1918, Gen. von Hoeppner sent Goering a congratulatory telegram.

'My flight at the start', 1917. Kilduff has added, 'Goering kept Albatros D.III 2049/16—seen here at far right—when he transferred from *Jasta* 26 to *Jasta* 27.'

'My fighters at the start at Bersee Airfield,' 1917. Kilduff has added, 'Line-up of *Jasta 27* aircraft at Iseghem, Belgium. Goering's Albatros D.V appears at far left, with the fuselage in black and not numbered, as were other *Staffel* aircraft.' Goering's *Jasta 27* Albatros D.V statistics: 'The fuselage was painted in black and white, but the wings retained the standard green and mauve camouflage. The serial number was D 1027. Type: single-seat fighter. Engine: Mercedes D.IIIa inline, 180-200 hp. Armament: Two Spandau machine guns. Speed: 116 mph at 3,280 feet. Climb: four minutes to 3,280 feet. Ceiling: 20,500 feet. Endurance: Two hours. Weight/empty: 1,511-2,061 pounds. Span: 29 feet, 8½ inches. Length: 24 feet ⅝ inches.'

Goering has used the same caption for this photo. On 22 April 1918, Goering's plane was blown by a gust of wind into a hangar. He was uninjured, but the plane was apparently retired from further aerial service.

'Our Appletree', Goering has called this 1917 Albatros view. On 31 May 1918, Gen. von Hoeppner approved the awarding of the Blue Max to Goering, citing, '... outstanding flying officer, who—by his reconnaissance and long range flights—... delivered exemplary support materials ... for critical decisions by his then commanders-in-chief ... Recovering from a serious wound, he again distinguished himself with personal daring in the latest great offensives of the 17th and 4th Armies as the leader of a *Jagdstaffel* [Fighter Squadron], which—under his prudent leadership—attained 49 aerial victories. He alone conquered 18 enemies in aerial combats.'

'A plane being repaired', 1917, is Goering's caption. On 3 July 1918, Goering—in concert with other top 'Blue Max' recipients—was testing new planes at the Adlershof Aircraft Test Establishment, outside Berlin.

Goering wrote of this scene of 8 June 1917, 'In front of my new fighter plane after launching the attack'. In July 1918, Goering went on leave for five weeks, returning to take command of *JG 1* on 22 August 1918.

Repairing a shot-up Albatros aircraft, 1917, with Goering possibly in the cockpit. Goering was cited as 'a leader of proved worth'. His final combat aircraft was an all-white Fokker D.VII, according to Kilduff.

'Me after a flight', Goering notes of this 1917 scene. As commander of the 'Flying Circus' in 1918, Goering found himself opposite the US 1st Army at St Mihiel in France, but he never shot down any US aircraft.

Goering's caption is 'At the start', 1917. In his final report as leader of *JG 1* in 1918, he remarked on 'the overwhelming tide of Allied troops'. The final combat of the 'Flying Circus' took place on 6 November 1918 in Eastern France, five days before the Armistice was concluded with the Allies.

'Albatros D.IV in flight, left turn,' Goering wrote in 1917.

Signature of Hermann Goering, 1918. After the Armistice, *JG 1*'s gear and equipment was returned to Germany by unit adjutant Karl Bodenschatz in 46 trucks, according to Kilduff, while Goering and his pilots flew ahead in their aircraft, during its final flight, to Darmstadt on 11 November 1918, the very day that 'the war to end all wars' ended.

Above left: 'In the garden,' 1916, Goering wrote of himself in this younger, slimmer mode than he later became noted for. He wears his Iron Cross above the Imperial Flying Service Badge.

Above right: Goering's caption reads, 'As the new Jagdstaffel/Jasta leader', 1917. Late in 1918, he asserted, 'I will never surrender to the Yanks!' but did, finally, in May 1945.

'In the garden', 1917. Goering later termed one aerial fight over Flanders in Belgium as 'a mad witches' sabbath in the skies'.

Above left: 'In Colmar', 1917: Goering with his walking cane. He wore the Iron Cross (right) on his tunic. According to Kilduff, after the Second World War, Luftwaffe *Generalleutnant* Hermann Dahlmann asserted that he was 'dubious ... of Goering's qualities, both as a flier and an officer', a truly scathing indictment from a former colleague.

Above right: 'Easter', 1917: Goering with the same cane.

Goering's caption is 'In English leather coat', 1917. This time he wields a lighter colored cane.

Above left: A dashing Hermann Goering displays an early predilection for full-length, fur-lined overcoats in occupied-France during the First World War. There would be many more during the glory years of the Nazi Third Reich later.

Above right: 'Morning toilet at the train', 1917.

Kilduff has captioned this photo, 'Always interested in showing his personal status, Goering took this photograph of the stately old house he lived in while based at Vouziers.'

Goering at ease, reading.

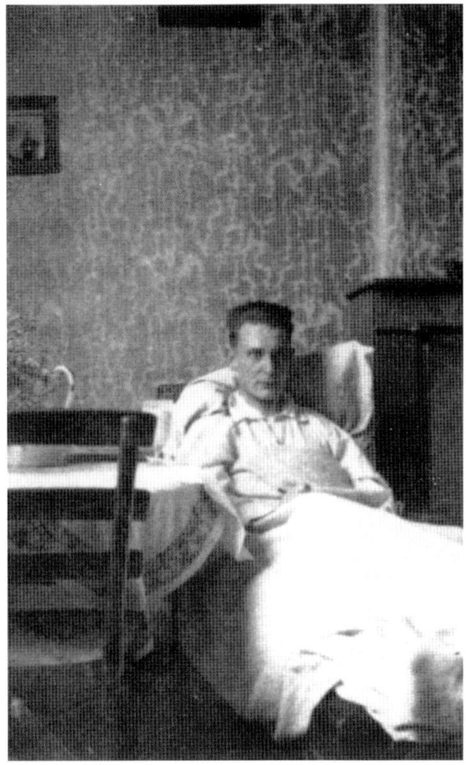

'In the wheelchair', 1917.

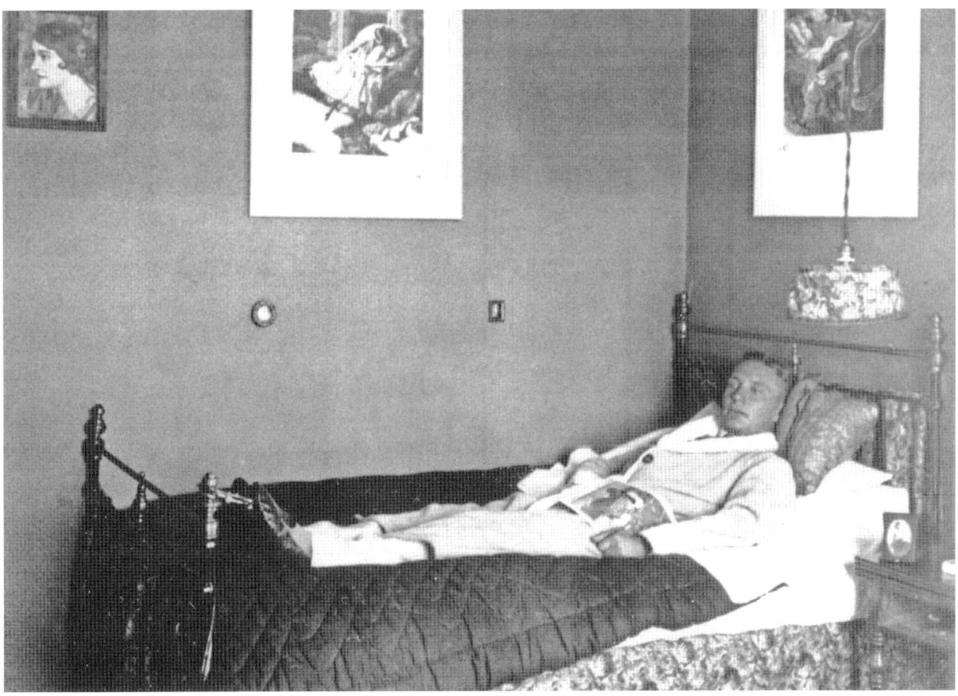

Goering's bedroom, 1917.

Above left: This Sanke postcard caption reads, 'Our successful battle flier, 1st L. Goering.' He wears the 'Blue Max' at the throat, the Iron Cross 2nd Class silver and black ribbon in his tunic buttonhole, the Iron Cross 1st Class at right above the Imperial Aviator's Badge below that, and the Wound Badge at right.

Above middle: 'The fighter pilot of the Great War' reads the caption of this photo that ran in a German Luftwaffe magazine in the Second World War. Note Goering's leg puttees.

Above right: A dashing Hermann Goering in late 1918, while commander of *JG 1*.

Above and below: 'Me studying in the map room', 1918, Goering wrote of this trio of him in a pensive mood. Manvell and Fraenkel note, 'By 1917, Goering's photographs could be bought in the shops ...'

Future Nazi Party politician Hermann Goering cradles a baby in this Great War photo from his albums. The child's identity is unknown. In 1918, Goering protested his last official orders from above: 'They are orders that I do not propose to obey! I will allow neither my men nor my machines to fall into the hands of the enemy. We cannot stay here and fight on, but we can make sure that when the end comes, we will be in Germany. The unit will evacuate its records and valuable equipment to Darmstadt forthwith. Tents and useless machines will be left behind. As for our planes, we will fly them out—to Darmstadt!'

5

Karl Bodenschatz: Adjutant to Both Von Richthofen and Goering 1890–1979

Charles Hamilton, author of the superb work *Leaders & Personalities of the Third Reich*, described Karl Bodenschatz as follows:

> Luftwaffe general and Goering's chief of staff. Born in Rehau, Upper Franconia on December 10, 1890, Bodenschatz served as the adjutant to Baron Manfred von Richthofen and Hermann Goering.
>
> On July 20, 1944, he was acting as Goering's liaison officer at [Führer] Headquarters and was severely injured in the [Army] bomb attempt on Hitler's life. Bodenschatz survived the war, and spent his final years in peaceful retirement. He died in Erlangen on August 25, 1979.

Thus, this is the bare bones of the much overlooked life and career of Karl Bodenschatz!

In their 1982 biographical sketch entitled 'Adjutant Karl Bodenschatz, Jagdgeschwader 1' in *Cross & Cockade Journal*, writers George H. Williams and Marvin L. Skelton performed stellar work in fleshing out his résumé thus:

> In mid-1917—while serving as adjutant of *Jasta Boelcke*, 1st Lt Karl Bodenschatz was personally selected by ... von Richthofen to furnish the administrative skills so vital to the success of *JG 1*.
>
> Although Karl Bodenschatz is best remembered for this duty, it was but one of a series of assignments and, in all, he served as a professional soldier—without interruption—from 1910-45 ...
>
> One of the most valuable parts of *Jagd in Flanderns Himmel/Hunting in Flanders Skies* (1935) is the highly detailed War Diary kept by Bodenschatz, as adjutant ...

The Bodenschatz version of Goering's appointment to lead the 'Flying Circus'

Here is how Bodenschatz described this all-important event in Goering's life in his 1935 book, republished in an English edition in 1998 as *Hunting with Richthofen* (for which Goering himself—again his superior, this time in the new Luftwaffe—wrote the Foreword):

> On the evening of July 3, 1918 the *Geschwader* adjutant [Bodenschatz himself] went pensively into the commander's room and took into his safekeeping the *Geschwaderstock*, the stick with the thick knob that Richthofen and Reinhard had both carried. Who was to carry it now? What would be the name of the new commander? Into whose hands was the ace card of the German Air Service—the *Jagdgeschwader* Richthofen—to be given?
>
> The adjutant was not the only one pondering the answer. The personnel adviser to the Commanding General of the Air Service [Gen. Hoeppner] was racking his brains over it as well. The selection of candidates was not very large. *JG Richthofen* had to get a first-rate man. The new *JG 2* and *3* were led by Capt. Rudolf Berthold and 1st Lt Bruno Lörzer [who was thus a candidate for the post himself, in effect in rivalry with his old friend, Goering].
>
> These two mustn't be recalled, but who should get *JG 1*? Who should be Richthofen's heir?
>
> In five days, the decision is made. In accordance with Order No. 178654 of the Commanding General of the Air Service—under the date of July 8, 1918—1st Lt Hermann Goering is appointed commander of the glorious *JG Richthofen*.
>
> The *Geschwader* breathes a sigh of relief. This man is not unknown to them. He is the splendid leader of *Jasta 27*, victor of 21 aerial combats, and wears the *Pour le Mérite*. He is the man who fulfils all of the requirements that will be tacitly placed on the commander of the first and most famous *JG* of the Army, by both his superiors and his subordinates.
>
> He is himself a first-rate fighter pilot, in a position to command the most daring fighter pilots of the Air Service, capable of putting these elite men into action together as a large unit against a numerical superiority of men and machines that was rapidly growing in every tactical aspect of the air war. The new commander was 'right', he was a 'personality …'
>
> On July 14th, the new commander arrived at the *Geschwader* in Beugneux. The impression he made met their high expectations in every respect. He was the finest type of young, active officer. In the quiet, well-proportioned features of his face there dwelt cold-bloodedness and energy. His eyes were clear, arresting, and calm, and when his face and eyes relaxed, one discovered the unerring common sense sparkling behind them.
>
> The man was tough. They saw that in the way he moved. They heard it in his words. It breathed from his very being. He had the *Geschwader* well in hand in no time …
>
> 1st Lt Goering's speech—short as it is—has an intense, illuminating power. It is not a prepared speech, but rather words formulated from the moment itself, and spoken in a strangely penetrating voice …

The adjutant—1st Lt Bodenschatz—presents the *Geschwaderstock* to the new commander. The wooden stick—that both Richthofen and Reinhard had carried—is now handed over to Goering with a few respectful and heartfelt words. It had been made by shop foreman Holzapfel for Richthofen in his day, and he had presented it to the Baron, who had taken real pleasure in this sturdy walking stick.

As the officers disperse, they are in agreement with each other and their new commander down to the last fibre of their beings. Here stands the right man in the right place at just the right time, 24 hours before the great offensive.

Goering reports

On 17 July 1918, the new commander sent in his first official report on the aerial combat situation to the 7th Army aviation commander:

> Up until now, only French air units appeared on the Front of the 7th Army. Since the beginning of the attack, powerful English reinforcements have arrived, numerous single-seater echelons in particular. In the area of the attack—especially in the Marne Valley between Méry and Dormans-Verneuil—enemy air activity that is numerically far superior, prevails in the afternoon and evening hours.
>
> The English single-seaters—generally in several strong flights staggered in altitude—give a good account of themselves in the good, old way. The French fighter pilots—on the other hand—only rarely venture over the Front, and avoid any serious combat. In contrast to this, the French two-seaters always appear in strong squadrons flying together.
>
> They carry out their bombing raids ruthlessly, partly at low altitudes. The twin-engine Caudrons are similar in this predilection. Experience has shown that their armour plating is not penetrated by our armour-piercing ammunition, even after repeated attempts. Armament consists of six machine guns (two sets of double machine guns in the back, two machine guns in front).
>
> The enemy Caudron squadrons carry out their orders without regard to German fighter pilots. On July 15, 1918, during an attack on a Caudron from close range, I myself fired almost all of my ammunition. The Caudron calmly flew on without worrying about me! A serious engagement with these armoured and well-armed aircraft would demand heavy sacrifices. The flak batteries must be called upon primarily for combating the Caudrons. They always fly close together, and thus present a favourable target for the anti-aircraft guns.
>
> The *Geschwader* was first put into action on the right flank of the Army for defence against the enemy air units advancing from the southwest. The superior enemy air operations on the battlefield south of the Marne (River) automatically drew the *Geschwader* into the attack area where our troops were fighting. The individual *Staffeln* were taking off, in parts, five times a day. The pilots and machines cannot provide this kind of effort indefinitely.
>
> Combining the *Staffeln* into a half-*Geschwader* and putting the whole *Geschwader* into action were very soon necessary. While the *Geschwader* was flying at the Front in these

stronger, closed formations, air mastery was assured. The enemy—who is numerically far stronger—can always send in fresh forces.

The enemy quite cleverly takes advantage of those moments when our fighter pilots are less numerous to venture cross our lines unexpectedly. Despite immediate takeoffs upon relatively quick incoming reports, only in rare cases have we been able to reach and combat these squadrons that have broken through in time. The laying of urgently needed lines must, at all costs, be always completed by the Army prior to the attack.

The *Geschwader* is well equipped with airplanes. The Fokker D.VII with the BMW engine is comparable—and in part superior—to the enemy airplanes. The Fokker D.VII with the high-compression Mercedes engine is a thoroughly comparable machine as well.

In the last few days, different aircraft have crashed in flames as a result of the easy ignition of the phosphorus ammunition. I have banned this ammunition. Remedy is urgently needed, since attacks on captive balloons are impossible until further notice.

Goering, 1st Lt and *Geschwader* Commander.

The very next day marked Goering's twenty-second and last aerial victory, as well as his first and only one as commander of *JG 1*. He reported on the action: 'On July 18, 1918, at 8.15 AM, I attacked a couple of Spads. I forced one Spad down and—after a dogfight—shot it down. It fell into a forested ravine near Bandry ...'

On 13 August 1918, according to Bodenschatz, this notice came from higher headquarters: 'Due to the heavy losses of the last few days, [the] *Geschwader* is condensed to one *Staffel*. Collaboration with *JG 3* and *Jagdgruppe* Greim.'

There was also a farewell telegram from Imperial German Crown Prince Wilhelm:

JG Richthofen is departing from my Army Group following glorious achievements! During its time with us, it has overcome 884 opponents. Under its active commander, it brought relief to the hard fighting troops on the ground—and in so doing—achieved its 500th air victory. My thanks and my appreciation go with the *JG* as it departs.

With particular joy, I have taken note of the fact that, on the day the *Geschwader* changed bases, it was able to actively intervene on the new Front, downing 13 of the enemy. Together with the *Geschwader*, I mourn the loss of brave comrades, in particular the loss of 1st Lt Löwenhardt, whose exemplary achievements will remain unforgettable.

Wilhelm, Crown Prince of Germany and of Prussia.

Karl Bodenschatz

Karl Bodenschatz was born in Rehau, Overfranken [Upper Franconia], Germany, on 10 December 1890 ... His father—Heinrich Bodenschatz—was a high school teacher. Karl Bodenschatz attended a liberal arts school in Hof/Saale, and was graduated in June 1910. He promptly enlisted in the 8th Royal Bavarian Infantry Regiment, and was a cadet at the War Academy in Metz until 1912. Also at the War Academy at Metz at this time was Cadet Oswald Boelcke of the Prussian Cadet Corps, and it is reasonable to assume that this later led to Bodenschatz being appointed adjutant for *Jasta 2*.

From Metz, Bodenschatz moved on to the officer's school at Münich, where he served as lieutenant, 1st lieutenant, battalion adjutant, and company commander … From the outbreak of hostilities in August 1914 until mid-1916, Lt Bodenschatz saw active combat service in the 8th Royal Bavarian Infantry Regiment.

During 1915–16, he took part in the difficult battles in the area around Verdun, including the storming of Forts Douaumont and Vaux … one of the most costly episodes in military history …

General der Flieger Karl Bodenschatz … recalled the period following the First World War:

> … I had the good fortune to be kept on … In 1927, I was ordered to visit the American Air Forces in Long Island, and the visit with my brothers and sister—who lived in the USA—was, for me, a great experience … I was a captain, major, company commander, and later a battalion commander.
>
> Personally, I sympathized with the pure German movement (Nazis), but I never joined the Party. In 1933, the Nazis took over power in the country. Goering—my last commander in the *JG Richthofen*—brought me to Berlin. He wanted me to become a bureaucrat and join the Party [*sic*], but I declined. I wanted to remain a soldier—and I remained one, too.
>
> The time up to the beginning of the Second World War was, indeed, the most interesting of my life. The building of the Luftwaffe of the Armed Forces was a huge task. It demanded of me constant association with the highest levels of the Reich (President, Supreme Commander of the Armed Forces, and of the Army and Navy) [i.e., first von Hindenburg, and then Hitler] with most of the government ministries, with diplomats, and leaders of the economy.
>
> As part of my duties, I had to visit all the European countries [with the exception of the Soviet Union]. The experience of my life grew richer and richer each year.
>
> The Second World War saw me without interruption as representative of the Supreme Commander of the Luftwaffe [Goering] to the Führer's Headquarters, in all theatres of the war. I witnessed difficult decisions that the Supreme Commander of the Armed Forces [Hitler] had to make.
>
> My military career ended on July 20, 1944. I was so badly wounded in the assassination attempt against Hitler that I still suffer today the effect of the wounds. I served as lieutenant colonel, colonel, major general, lieutenant general, and colonel general.

Bodenschatz suffered severe burns and other injuries, including considerable hearing loss. While he recovered from his injuries in the Zoo Bunker Hospital, one of his nurses was Mrs Erna Dziuba, whom he later married. At the end of the war, he surrendered to the Americans, and later testified on Goering's behalf at the trial held in Nuremberg before the International Military Tribunal between November 14, 1945 and September 1946 …

> I was a prisoner-of-war under the English and Americans. I endured this difficulty unbroken, and with proper behaviour. I was released from PoW status in July 1947 . . . I was body and soul a soldier! As a youth, I was interested in all things military. In my parents' home and in school, I was brought up as a Christian and as a patriot. I chose after high school graduation the profession of a military officer, the highest rank of a soldier.
>
> I was no nationalist, but a good patriot. With my soldiers and officers, I was a strict but proper commander. In that manner, I trained in peacetime young men for the defence of the nation. In war, I carried out my soldierly duty on all fronts.

Bodenschatz postwar

In 1919, Karl Bodenschatz married Maria Walter, and they had one son, Manfred. Maria Walter Bodenschatz died in 1960 ... In 1966, Karl Bodenschatz married Mrs Erna Dziuba, and his name was given to her son, Gerald, by mutual agreement ...

Services for Karl Bodenschatz were conducted on August 30, 1979 in Nuremberg. He was cremated, and the ashes later buried on October 19, 1979 in Waldfriedhof Cemetery in Münich. It is not only Gen. Bodenschatz' grave, but a family gravesite ...

In summary, it seems that Karl Bodenschatz had been ideally suited for the role that fate had dealt him—a professional soldier. He was a very methodical man, and always sure of his facts. In later life—whenever he found a book that mentioned his name—he would check the facts involving him and about which he had first-hand knowledge.

If this part was accurate, he would buy the book and read it. His mind was as clear as a bell up to the time of his death and—although in later life he would repeat the stories of his wounds on many occasions—this wasn't due to senility. In his own words, he had been 'body and soul a soldier'.

Gen. Bodenschatz played a unique transitional role in the air forces of both Kaiser and Führer over the course of empire, republic, and dictatorship in both peace and war—twice over! Thus, his inclusion in this study is fitting in all respects.

In addition, he outlived *all* of his contemporary—and far better known—aviator colleagues: two of the three pilots Richthofen, Goering, Lörzer, Greim, Wever, Jeschonnek, Kesselring, and Milch—no mean feat, that!

One fan that Bodenschatz did *not* have on 4 May 1945 was the last Chief of Staff of the Luftwaffe, Col. Gen. Karl Koller. His diary entry for that date read, 'Have they [the Americans] caught Bodenschatz, I wonder, or is he still playing the butler?' As a member of the Reich Marshal's inner circle, he—like Lörzer—had earned his own share of personal enemies, too.

1Lt Karl Heinrich Bodenschatz as the adjutant of *JG 1* in December 1917 at Avesnes-le-Sec—according to Diggens—holding a small dog and posing before a Fokker triplane. He served in turn all three commanders of this famed 'Flying Circus' unit: von Richthofen, Reinhard, and Goering. (*Bruno J. Schmaling Collection, C&CJ, Library of Congress*)

1Lt Bodenschatz of the 1st Bavarian Flying Company at the Military Flying Station at Oberschleissheim near Münich in 1912.

JG 1 adjutant Lt Bodenschatz with another dog, in front of a row of fighters. Note the engine cover on the closest one.

Unit adjutant Bodenschatz (left) and Col. Gotz, commanding officer of the 3rd Battalion, 8th Royal Bavarian Infantry Regiment on 17 June 1915. The black dog seated on the table was named Bally Lager.

From left to right: Lt Eggers, Bodenschatz with dog Joffre (named after the famous French Army Marshal Joseph Joffre), and 1Lt Otto Bernert at *Jasta Boelcke*, again with fighter planes on the flight line as the preferred backdrop.

From left to right: Bodenschatz in white tunic, ace Ernst Udet at center, and commanding officer of *Jasta Boelcke*, Karl Bolle, Fall, 1918.

Cadet Bodenschatz (second from right) at the Metz War Academy on 18 August 1910.

From left to right: Joachim Wolff pets a dog, watched by Bodenschatz, von Schönebeck, Lothar von Richthofen, and his older brother, Baron Manfred von Richthofen, who has the unit's famed *Geschwaderstock* at his side. Note the suspended ring that was used as the unit's alarm system.

The Red Baron and his adjutant visit *Jasta 10. From left to right:* Erich Löwenhardt, Bodenschatz, Kuhn, von Richthofen, Aloys Heldmann, Hugo Schaeffer, Paul Aue, and Justus Grassmann.

Jasta 26 in February 1917. From left to right, standing: Weckbrodt, Lange, Haussen, *Staffelführer* Bruno Lörzer, two unknown men, Goering wearing overcoat and with cane, Linke, Blume, Auer, and Rumpel. Sitting, left to right, are Fritz Lörzer and Wever. That May, Goering was posted as *Jasta 27 Staffelführer*, and on 5 July 1918 was named the third and last commander of *JG Baron von Richthofen 1*. Williams and Skelton in the Autumn 1982 issue of *Cross & Cockade Journal* noted, 'The slender officer who arrived to command *JG 1* in the summer of 1918 was far different from the later Goering … He was a strong, very competent, and courageous professional officer, a splendid organizer, and born leader—the very type of commander who would appeal to Bodenschatz, and it is believed that—for the remainder of their association—this was the image Bodenschatz served so well. Goering took over during the waning days of the war, as the tide inevitably turned against the Germans.'

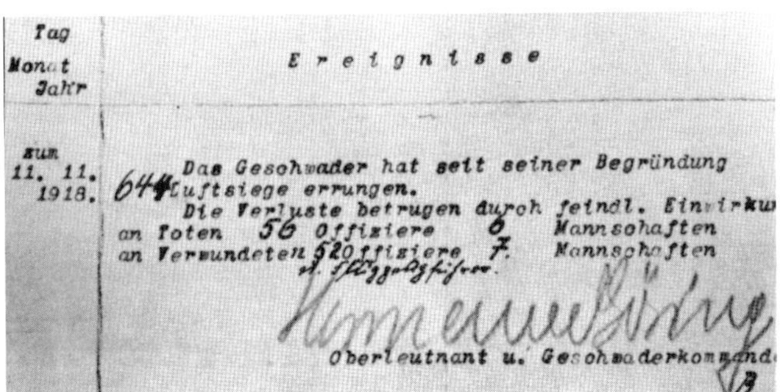

Tag
Monat
Jahr

Ereignisse

zum
11. 11.
1918.

Das Geschwader hat seit seiner Begründung
644 Luftsiege errungen.
Die Verluste betrugen durch feindl. Einwirku
an Toten 56 Offiziere 6 Mannschaften
an Verwundeten 52 Offiziere 7 Mannschaften

Oberleutnant u. Geschwaderkommand

Above left: 'One of Bodenschatz' final acts as adjutant of *JG 1* was to prepare and initial the following message, which Goering delivered orally to the assembled personnel: "The *Geschwader*, since its mobilization, has gained 644 aerial victories. Losses due to enemy action: Fatalities … 56 officers, 6 enlisted men. Wounded … 52 officers, 7 enlisted men. (Signed) Hermann Goering, 1st Lt and *Geschwader* Commander." '

Above right: Of this photo, Kilduff has noted, 'Goering's arrival [center] as the first air mail pilot of *Svenska Lufttrafik AB* at Malmö, Sweden, from Warnemünde via Copenhagen-Kastrup in August 1920, thereby opening the air mail service between Germany and Sweden.' Goering had made his first transitional step away from the famed aviator of the Great War into the future politician of the Nazi Party.

6

How Many Goering Kills? 1916–18

The 1965 Musciano tally

Oberleutnant/1st Lt Hermann Goering—*Jasta 26, 27*; *Jagd 1*
Victory numbers, dates, locations, and enemy planes are as follows:
1—December 1916, Nieuport Scout; 2—December 1916, BE.2c; 3—December 1916, BE.2c; 4—February 1917, BE.2c; 5—8 May 1917, Spad; 6—May 1917, Spad; 7—24 May 1917, Spad; 8—8 June 1917, Nieuport Scout; 9—15 June 1917; FE.2d; 10—15 June 1917, Camel; 11—5 July 1917, Ypres, Sopwith; 12, 13, 14, 15—21 October 1917, Linselles, Sopwith; 16, 17—21 February 1918, SE.5; 18—May 1918, BE; 19—May 1918, Camel; 20—24 June 1918, SE.5; 21—24 June 1918, SE.5; 22—18 July 1918; Spad.

The 1997 Franks-Giblin tally

> It is quite impossible to deal with any aspect of Hermann Goering's early adult life without bringing to the subject the inevitable preconceptions formed and colored by a knowledge of his subsequent life and career. Equally, it is impossible not to reflect upon the fateful irony that allowed him to survive the Great War when so many good men died in that terrible conflict.
>
> Or does that do him an injustice? Was he—in those early days at least—just another brave young man flying and fighting for his country in a war that destroyed so many brilliant futures? Certainly, he enjoyed signal success, gaining the approbation of his Kaiser and rising to command Imperial Germany's premier air fighting unit, *Jagdgeschwader 1*.
>
> And yet, and yet, and yet ...!
>
> Those who try know full well the difficulties surrounding the retrospective research into combat claims and the identification of the men on the wrong end of the so-called 'victories'.
>
> However—even given all of the usual problems associated with the subject—we cannot help but be struck by the recurring inconsistencies attending so many of Goering's victories. The claims were undoubtedly contemporary and owed nothing to his eventual attainment

of power and influence, and it is generally accepted that the Imperial German Air Service's system for the confirmation recording of claims was thorough and, usually, impartial.

Yet contrary to the high and exactly standards, Goering's claims frequently appear to be inadequately founded and generally unsubstantiated—significantly more so than any of the other aces' claims. Why?

Is this early evidence of an ambitious, forceful, and devious personality that was able to bend and manipulate events and people to his own advantage? Or is this just a trite conclusion colored by hindsight?

Victory No. 1: 16 November 1916, Farman, Tahure, 2.30 PM

Pilot Goering had Lt Bernert as observer flying in Albatros C 486/15 on a photo reconnaissance mission when Goering allegedly shot down a French Farman aircraft.

In 1997, the authors asserted:

> The victim's identity remains unclear even to this day as—so far as can be established—the French suffered no combat losses on the day—in fact, not even a single Caudron appears to have been lost in the whole of the month.

Pilot Goering suffered a knee injury on 14 December 1915 after a crash in Germany, but he returned to flying 'several times a day, every day', both the Albatros two-seater and also the AEG G.II twin-engine, three-seater aircraft.

Victory No. 2: 14 March 1916, Caudron, SE Haumont Wood, noon

Pilot Goering was accompanied by Observer Count von Schaesberg and Gunner Boje in three-seater AEG G.II G19/15 on a brief photo reconnaissance mission when they encountered a trio of 'Caudron types'. Goering forced one down behind German lines and witnessed ground troops taking prisoner the crew of the aircraft. 'The French report two losses ... both of them Caudrons' and one of them was reported missing.

In 'constant' action throughout March-July 1916, Goering started flying a single-seat Halberstadt D.III, then transferred from Stenay to Jametz to FAA 203 single-seat Scout fighter unit, leading to his third 'kill'.

Victory No. 3: 30 July 1916, Caudron, Mamey, 10.30 AM

Goering piloted a Halberstadt Scout against five twin-engine Caudrons, 'with Goering claiming to have dispatched quickly one of the French machines ... A Voisin ... did fail to return.'

That August, Goering was back with FFA 25 piloting single-seaters, until the unit was disbanded on the 14th, and he transferred to the Metz *Kampfstaffel* (Fighter

Squadron). In September he joined *Jasta 7*, and then went with Lörzer to *Jasta 5* at Gonnelieu near Cambrai during the Battle of the Somme. Wounded on 2 November 1916 in the right hip, Goering was hospitalized for weeks in both France and Münich, then being posted for 'light duties' around Christmas 1916 to FEA 10.

He visited *Jasta 26* in January 1917, and was ordered there on 15 February, flying the Albatros D.III Scout.

Victory No. 4: 23 April 1917, FE.2b A823, Squadron 18, 5.20 PM

Over Barelle flying Albatros D.III 2049/16, Goering attacked four FE.2b aircraft on a night bombing raid. The enemy pilot landed the 'burning' plane behind British lines near Arras.

Victory No. 5: 28 April 1917, Sopwith 1½ Strutter, St Quentin, 6.30 PM

> [Flying the same plane again, Goering] ran into a flight of six Sopwith two-seaters ... The nationality of Goering's claimed victory is impossible to ascertain ... Only one Royal Flying Corps Sopwith was lost on that day ... There were no French losses on that day, and despite Goering's assertion that his victim fell inside German lines (which should have helped to make identification simple) still this claim remains less than clear cut.

Victory No. 6: 29 April 1917, Nieuport XVII N3192, Naval Squadron 6, 7.45 PM

Again Goering flew the same aircraft in a trio of sorties on this single day, winning his sixth victory on the third one, wounding the enemy pilot in the calf and forcing him down behind German lines. The pilot became a PoW. Goering was himself attacked returning to base at Bohain when his lateral controls were damaged, but he landed safely. His attacker was himself shot down, but remains unidentified. Lörzer may have been the winning pilot in this engagement within a fight, shooting down the pilot who attacked Goering.

Victory No. 7: 10 May 1917, DH.4? Le Pavé, 3.05 PM

Goering reported that this win was over a British triplane, but it was probably a DH.4 biplane bomber in fact. However, 'There were no reported British triplane losses on this day ... yet another unsatisfactory situation that defies explanation ... Once again, the surviving records are irreconcilable with the circumstances of his claim.'

Nevertheless, Goering was promoted to *Staffelführer* of *Jasta 27*, 'with five years' service behind him'. The new command was located at Ghistelles opposite Ypres on the German 4th Army Front. 'Goering insisted on taking his favorite Albatros 2049/16 with him over the border to Belgium.'

Victory No. 8: 8 June 1917, Nieuport XVII B1656, Squadron 1, 7.30 AM

Leading four of his new pilots on a fighter patrol, Goering encountered an enemy patrol and forced his opponent into a crash landing, where the plane 'burst into flames'. The pilot survived and was captured. This was Goering's famous victory over RFC 2Lt Frank Dilloway Slee, described earlier. Slee died in 1967 at Bunbury, Western Australia.

Victory No. 9: 16 July 1917, SE.5 A8931, Squadron 56, 8.10 PM

This victory 'almost cost him his life' in combat against RFC 2Lt Robert Gordon Jardine, 'the two exchanging fire at a range of 50 yards before breaking off'. Again flying Albatros 2049/16, Goering had trouble with his engine, and 'Jardine's oil tank was smashed'.

Goering was sent spinning down toward earth, but leveled out before he made a hard landing; Lt Jardine claimed that his opponent crashed, but he, too, was forced to land behind his own lines. 'He, too, turned his machine over, the fuselage breaking in half behind the cockpit. Both machines were wrecked and would never fly again—the end of Goering's beloved 2049/16 ... Both sides could claim with equal veracity a confirmed victory—in soccer parlance, a score draw!'

Lt Jardine was killed in another dogfight, aged 30, four days later by another German pilot.

Victory No. 10: 24 July 1917, Martinsyde G100, Passchendaele, 8.45 PM

> Yet another 'phantasmal' Goering claim? Not only were no Martinsyde G100s reported lost on this day, but, indeed, none were even reported damaged ... Goering not only identified his victim as a Martinsyde 'Flying Elephant' but claimed that after it fell on the Allied side of the lines ... he circled it several times before flying home ... Furthermore, there were no Belgian aircraft of any type lost on this day.

Victory No. 11: 5 August 1917, Sopwith Camel B3792, Squadron 70, 8.15 PM

'Many of Goering's successes occurred in the evening hours,' the authors assert, 'and this proved to be no exception.' His new Albatros Scout ran into Sopwith Camels, and he attacked one immediately, 'firing at a range of no more than 50 meters. According to Goering, flames became to come from the Sopwith and—trailing smoke—it went into a spin and was lost in a cloud.'

He was given credit for the kill on 29 August 1917. The enemy pilot died on 12 June 1953, aged 62—like Slee, outliving Goering.

Victory No. 12: 25 August 1917, Sopwith Camel B3918, Squadron 70, 8.40 PM

This was another evening victory for Hermann Goering. Struggling with a gun jam, he sighted a single Sopwith Camel and engaged it from above. 'It disappeared, crashing into the haze,' he reported, while he had to engage a triplane in the meantime. 'His "victim" did not crash;' wounded, he got his plane back home. It was sent off for repair, and he died of blood poisoning in London on 21 December 1931.

Victory No. 13: 3 September 1917, DH.4? north of Lampernisse, 9 AM

Yet more difficulties attend the circumstances of this 'victory'. Goering flew Albatros 4424/17 to help engage seven Spads and five two-seaters, and 'claimed a two-seater downed in an area southwest of Dixmude, the machine falling behind the Allied lines'. The authors call Goering's after-action report 'confusing and ambiguous', and say that he did, indeed, engage two planes, but, 'For sure, neither of the two British machines were shot down ... In summation, even with the closest possible examination of events, it is just not possible to a match a victim with this claimed Goering "victory"!'

Victory No. 14: 21 September 1917, Bristol FE.2b A7224, Squadron 48, 9.05 AM

Goering was again flying 4424/17 leading a patrol that met fourteen British aircraft. Goering's bullets killed the 29-year-old pilot, but he did not die before landing the plane near Sleyhage.

On 20 October 1917, Lt Goering was awarded the Hohenzollern House Order.

Victory No. 15: 21 October 1917, SE.5a B547, Squadron 84, 3.45 PM

Now flying Albatros D.V 2159/17, *Staffelführer* Goering again ran into opposing Sopwiths. He shot down one, and helped shoot down a second, but was credited only with the first.

Victory No. 16: 7 November 1917, DH.5, north-west of Poelcapelle, 9.15 AM

> Confusion again. The German ... records this victory as occurring 12 hours after it actually took place [with Goering flying 2153/17] leading nine of his command. They engaged four DH.5s, one of which apparently Goering claimed he shot down, the machine falling behind the Allied lines ...
>
> The problem with the claim is that there was only one British 'casualty' this day ... and that occurred in the early afternoon, hours after Goering's DH.5 'victory'! An appraisal of all the possibilities ... throws up nothing that could remotely substantiate Goering's claim.

Victory No. 17: 21 February 1918, SE.5A C5325, Squadron 60, 10 AM

This is the famous fight described in the 1933 British *Popular Flying* article that carried Goering's byline, as we have seen. The authors conclude:

> The probability is that some sycophant wrote up this rubbish to enhance the reputation of the new Minister, but the certainty is that Goering gave it his blessing.
>
> The mysterious Capt. was, in fact, Lt George Barton Craig, a Canadian who most certainly put up a good fight—he was an experienced pilot—but would not have recognized himself from Goering's description, as being 'famous!' ... Craig was certainly not dead when they took him from his machine, as he surely would have been with 'three bullets in his head and seven more through his body'!
>
> The two SE.5As almost certainly accidentally collided with each other, and were not shot down by anybody.

Lt Craig, 23, was buried in Belgium, and thus his fate was known at the time, and especially by 1933. The editors gave Goering a pass by stating otherwise at the end of his article, I conclude.

Victory No. 18: 7 April 1918, RE.8 B876, Squadron 42, 12.50 PM

This win against the Royal Flying Corps occurred seventeen days into the famous Kaiser's Battle of March 1918 on the Western Front, with Goering chasing and then shooting down a two-seater observation plane behind British lines.

With just eighteen victories—he was two short of the twenty then required for the award of the 'Blue Max'—'But receive it he did on June 2, 1918,' and the next day he and his *Jasta 27* were relocated back to the French front at Mont de Soissons Ferme.

Victory No. 19: 5 June 1918, AR.2?, Vivières, 10 AM

This time, Goering's foe was a plane co-ordinating artillery fire as he himself used to do.

> French ground troops poured fire up at his triplane as he circled the wreck ... French records show two Breguet XIVs lost on this day, but no AR.2s. We assume, therefore, that one of these was Goering's 19th victim.

Victory No. 20: 9 June 1918, Spad 1, Spa 94, 8.45 AM

Firing from his new Fokker D.VII 324/18 fighter, Goering shot down a French single-seater behind German lines.

Victory No. 21: 17 June 1918, Spad 1, Spa 93, 8.30 AM

Goering led seven aircraft of his *Jasta 27* to fight five French aircraft west of Soissons, and 'fired 500 rounds into his hapless victim. The stricken Spad fell away and crashed by the side of a small wood ...' The pilot was captured.

On 11 June 1918, Goering was told that he was being given command of the famous 'Flying Circus', *JG 1*. 'The appointment suggests that he was not without friends in high places!' Imperial German Crown Prince Wilhelm? *Ritter* von Epenstein? Both? Neither? We simply don't know for sure, but that is my own conclusion.

> It was true that he had been in almost continuous combat for the whole of the war [an assertion that was not true, as we have seen earlier], that he was a professional, regular soldier with 21 victories and long experience of command, but were there not others even more qualified? In this—as in most walks of life—patronage and influence are powerful allies ...

Victory No. 22: 18 July 1918, Spad 1, Spa ? 8.15 AM

Flying Fokker D.VII 194/18, Goering attacked two single-seater aircraft, shooting one down that fell into a wooded ravine, his sole victory as 'Flying Circus' commander, and also his very last one.

> He had been amazingly lucky so far ... To be fair, it must be said that Hermann Goering was popular with the men under his command—there was no doubt that they regarded their leader not just with respect, but with affection. Goering went on leave on July 22nd, returning almost a month later on August 22nd.
>
> On September 2nd, he was called to attend GHQ for two days and, perhaps surprisingly, took leave again on October 22nd ... The end was nigh ... He is remembered now not as

one of the elite band of early military fliers, but as one of the perpetrators of crimes that have rarely been paralleled in human history.

Hermann Goering's death—by his own hand—came on October 15, 1946, some 28 years after the end of his own fighting war. Found guilty of crimes against humanity by the Allies, his request to be executed by firing squad was denied. Cunning as ever, Goering used a cleverly concealed phial of cyanide to cheat the hangman; he was 53 years old.

The 2010 Kilduff tally
Goering's first aerial victory, 16 November 1915

Pilot Goering flew with Observer Lt Bernert in Albatros C.1 C 486/15. They were attacked by a French Farman biplane:

> German ground observers reported seeing the French aeroplane fall from the sky ... Whether the Farman claimed ... was destroyed or put out of commission is questionable, as French records show no air combat losses at all that day.

Goering's second victory, 14 March 1916

Goering flew an AEG G.II with Observer Julius Count von Schaesberg-Thannheim and Gunner Boje when they came under attack by three French Caudron G.4 two-seater, two-engine aircraft. In his after-action report, the Count claimed that Goering forced it down. All three crew members received credit for the downing, 'even though Goering ... was unarmed and, thus, had not fired a shot'.

Goering's third victory, 30 July 1916

General of Infantry Adolf von Oven's report of this action underlined Goering's aerial defense of Metz, and also confirmed his third kill:

> ... Lt Goering attacked five aeroplanes from an enemy formation over La Cote ... He brought one of the enemy aeroplanes—a two-engine Caudron—crashing down ... I convey to Lt Goering my complete appreciation and my thanks for his repeatedly outstanding conduct here.

Goering's fourth victory, 23 April 1917

'Goering shot down a rear-engine British FE.2b.' The plane returned to its own lines, where it reportedly crashed, and Goering was credited. Goering's own combat report reads, 'After a short fight, I set fire to the opponent.' The British reported that the downed airplane was junked.

Goering's fifth victory, 28 April 1917

Goering wrote of this fight, 'About 6.30 PM … aerial combat with …six Sopwiths over St Quentin. I shot down one Sopwith, which crashed behind our lines.' The crew was captured.

Goering's sixth victory, 29 April 1917

Kilduff asserts that there was no doubt that Goering downed a Nieuport, just as the pilot claimed in his after-action report: '… Aerial combat over Ramicourt with a Nieuport single-seat fighter. I shot it down … tumbled over on landing.' The wounded pilot survived.

Goering's seventh victory, 10 May 1917

Goering downed an Airco DH.4 two-seat recon. and bomber.

In 1923, Goering noted in a German airmen's experience anthology:

> … I catch sight of the enemy: four big bombers hastening back to their frontlines … Several single-seat fighters are advancing …to cover them … We hurry after the bombers in a dive … I charge into the formation … Fierce machine-gun fire from four aeroplanes crackles towards me … The smoke streaks of the incendiary ammunition come whistling close by me … I still have one opponent to deal with. Infuriated, he hurls his bullets at me. I dive below him, and gain momentum so that I can pursue him like an arrow.
>
> The enemy observer stretches far out of his cockpit to be able to shoot more easily at me; just then, I also open fire. At the same time, my two machine guns hurl a hail of metal into the enemy aeroplane. From 30-50 metres' distance, I am now right at his fuselage, while his stream of fire comes right by me, but I do not let up, and soon the observer slumps over.
>
> Just after that, an enormous flame of fire bursts out of the machine and … the enemy aeroplane explodes … The flaming fuselage and its crew plunge to the ground. The wings break off … The enemy is demolished … It hits the ground and smashes to pieces.

His claim was approved, and Kilduff concurs.

Goering's eighth victory, 8 June 1917

In a 1920 anthology, Goering recalled:

> … Above us appeared a Nieuport formation of 12 units … small, silver-grey fighting machines … dived onto us. The … battle began … Suddenly, I see an opponent above me … He stalks me from out of the sun in order to surprise me and shoot me down from behind … The duel can begin … and he comes down on me like a hawk …

> I push my machine down a bit to pick up momentum, pull it around in a flash, and powerfully rise up towards him, at the same time opening fire with both machine guns. Instead of him catching me from behind and surprising me, I hit him from the front and parry his thrust, surprising him … My burst of fire is on the mark, for immediately he goes into a spin to get away from it … and now I am on his heels and forcing him down with my machine-gun fire … Often, we rush so closely by each other that we believe we are going to crash into each other.
>
> The Englishman fires splendidly, skilfully, and smartly. I see him clearly, sitting in his machine. The battle is furious, exciting, and strenuous … I skid into a turn, and my opponent has already spotted his advantage, and in a rage pounds away at me with his weapons. Several hits strike my aeroplane close behind me … He has also taken some hits.
>
> … He defends himself desperately … At extremely close range, I drive my shots into his machine. He goes tumbling down, his engine is off; he is shot to pieces … The landing goes badly, and his machine is smashed to bits. He himself is hurled out, but remains uninjured. The victory is finally mine, and the Englishman is taken prisoner …
>
> It was a tough struggle. The gruelling battle lasted 10 minutes.

This was the famous fight with Slee, but it was only when Slee read the 1951 Frischauer biography of Goering that he finally learned that his very first mission and fight had been with Hermann Goering, the famous Nazi Reich Marshal.

After this fight, Goering's picture appeared on Sanke postcard No. 535, just like the Red Baron. He had thus 'arrived'.

Goering's ninth victory, 16 July 1917

This was the famous fight in which Goering flew an Albatros D.III and killed 2Lt Robert G. Jardine.

In his after-action report, Goering wrote:

> I attacked a single-seater formation, and shot down one, which … crashed … I had to turn against a second opponent … As a result of that aerial combat, suddenly the engine dropped off its mountings … I immediately went into a spin … land[ed] the machine … where I nosed over … The second opponent got away.

Thus, Goering himself had been forced down. His plane—2049/16—was junked, and he got a new one, an Albatros D.V.

Goering's tenth victory, 24 July 1917

Of this win, Goering noted, 'I attacked the enemy machines … I cornered my opponent—apparently a Martinsyde—which I forced down in a spiral fight. The opponent spun often, and lastly crashed.'

Kilduff counters, 'The British ... recorded no casualties of Martinsyde or any other two-seaters in the area ... that day. Yet, Goering was credited with his 10th victory.'

Goering's eleventh victory, 5 August 1917

Goering's unit was assaulted by nine Sopwith F.1 Camels. From behind one of them, Goering opened up with a blast from 50 meters' range: 'Suddenly, flames ... and heavy smoke came out of the machine,' he wrote, 'and the opponent went down into a deep spiral in the dense cloud mass.'

His wounded opponent returned for a crash landing behind British lines, and survived.

Goering's twelfth victory, 25 August 1917

Goering broke off an initial pursuit when his twin Spandau machine guns jammed, but then attacked another Sopwith Camel after he had cleared them. He noted that this foe, 'fell downward, turning over several times, and rearing up ... crashed in the haze'.

His wounded foe survived, and Goering was credited with the win.

Goering's thirteenth victory, 3 September 1917

This was a controversial win over an Airco DH.4 two-seater.

Goering's fourteenth victory, 21 September 1917

Goering flew Albatros D.V 4424/17 with 'a black fuselage, white nose, and white tail'. He later wrote:

> I sighted an enemy formation of 14 units [bombers] ... I positioned myself closely below the tail of an opponent and opened fire at it ... The aeroplane crashed. Pilot and observer were injured. The machine was completely destroyed.

He was credited.

Goering's fifteenth victory, 21 October 1917

Witnessing five Sopwiths attacking a German LVG two-seat reconnaissance plane, Goering went to its assistance, downing one of the enemies north of Lille, a victory that Kilduff terms as 'reasonably certain'. The pilot became a German PoW.

Goering's sixteenth victory, 7 November 1917

At the head of nine Albatros fighters, Goering saw four Airco DH.5 fighters and shot down one behind British lines. He was awarded the victory claim.

Goering's seventeenth victory, 21 February 1918

This win was over an SE.5 fighter, as described in his famous *Popular Flying* article already run, the fight with Lt Craig. Kilduff terms this article as Goering's 'characteristic hyperbole'. He also states, 'Research shows that Craig and Kent collided, and may not have been shot down by Goering and Klimke at all.'

Goering's eighteenth victory, 7 April 1918

Again leading nine of his comrades, Goering assaulted a British RE.8 two-seater reconnaissance and fighter plane, 'within' British lines, aided by a second German fighter. Both enemy pilot and observer had machine guns. The Germans prevailed, the pilot was uninjured, but the observer was wounded.

Goering alone was credited with the kill.

Goering's nineteenth victory, 5 June 1918

His new Fokker D.VII fighter 278/18, had 'a white engine cowling and tail'. Flying it, Goering attacked a French AR.1 artillery spotter aircraft, and shot it down with 240 rounds of ammo, a win witnessed by his other aerial colleagues. However, Kilduff writes, 'In this author's view, it is not possible to validate or discount this victory claim, as Goering may have shot down this two-seater reconnaissance aircraft.'

Goering's twentieth victory, 9 June 1918

Goering flew Fokker D.VII 324/18 against a French Spad SVII, reporting that it 'dropped straight down like a stone and hit the ground', its pilot being captured. This win, too, was credited to Goering.

Goering's twenty-first victory, 17 June 1918

Goering's own after-action combat report noted:

> ... I spotted five Spads ... attacking our tethered balloons west of Soissons ... I came down and attacked them ... From 500 metres, I downed a 200-hp Spad that crashed ... Two of my Fokkers collided and crashed. Due to our attack, the tethered balloons remained unharmed.

Goering's twenty-second victory, 18 July 1918

Goering had yet another new Fokker D.VII, F294/18, 'painted yellow from the mid-point of the cockpit to the rudder ... the forward part of the fuselage was painted red', in remembrance of the slain Red Baron, shot down on 21 April 1918.

Goering recalled, 'I attacked some Spads. I pressed one downward and ... shot it down. It fell into a wooded ravine.'

It was his last aerial victory, but not for Lörzer, who continued gaining victories into September 1918. Lörzer thus ended the Great War with forty-four wins, exactly double that of his protégé—and later superior—Hermann Goering.

What was Hermann Goering's final tally?

That is the question Kilduff poses at the end of his own marvelous work:

> ... Some of his victory claims were questionable. Further, accounts by his contemporaries, Bruno Lörzer and Rudolf Nebel ... challenge the overall veracity of German fighter claims. Together, these factors add weight to the question: How many aircraft did Goering truly shoot or force down?
>
> A case by case examination shows that—given the method of awarding credit at the times of Goering's 22 victories—at best, he accounted for 18 or 19 enemy aircraft between November 16, 1915 and July 18, 1918 ...
>
> In view of the evidence currently at hand, Goering's first, 10th, and 16th victory claims seem less likely to have been graced by success, and his 19th was tenuous at best.

As near as I can determine from Franks and Giblin (1997), Goering personally may have killed ten men, wounded six, and caused the capture of seven. According to Kilduff (2010)—again, as near as I can make out—his comparative figures are four killed, six wounded, and four captured.

Goering's caption is 'Colmar airfield', 1917.

'Start at north Colmar', 1917.

'Stadtinneres von Rethel', 1915. With dog and swagger stick.

Lt Otto Konnecke, 'Blue Max' holder, credited with thirty-five aerial kills (left), with unknown officer at right.

Left to right: 'Assistant Dr Drouven, Sgt. Linke, and Reserve Lt Hansen', wrote Goering of these three 1917 portraits.

One of Goering's 1918 rivals for command of *JG 1* was Erich Löwenhardt (1897–1918) of *Jasta 10*, who ended the Great War with fifty-four victories and was another holder of the 'Blue Max'. He is seen here also wearing the Iron Cross and Imperial Pilot's Badge at right on his tunic.

'My (Spandau) machine guns being loaded with bullets' is Goering's caption to this shot.

'*Ehrenbecher dem Sieger im Luftkampfe*, the trophy given airmen for their first victory,' notes O'Connor of this photo of the Germanic eagle (top) triumphing over an Allied bird underneath it.

Goering captions these twin views—left and right—of the same aircraft 'Headstand', possibly an Albatros B.I biplane.

A 1917 'Headstand', lens man Goering wrote of this Albatros.

'[Lt Karl] Wewer's headstand with [Albatros] D.III', wrote Goering of these 1917 top and bottom views.

From left to right: Kurt Wusthoff, Werner Voss, Baron Manfred von Richthofen, Erich Löwenhardt, and Lothar von Richthofen, the Red Baron's younger brother and an ace in his own right.

Above left: Formal portrait of Lothar von Richthofen by Berlin photographer von Dühren. He wore his 'Blue Max' at the throat. When *JG 1* commander Lt Goering went on leave after achieving his twenty-second and last kill on 18 July 1918, he left the new Baron von Richthofen and fellow ace Ernst Udet, with sixty-two kills, in charge.

Above right: Ernst Udet (1896–1941), not Goering, was considered by many to be the logical successor to the Red Baron as commander of the 'Flying Circus'. Asher Lee writes, 'There is little doubt that Goering's combat record and skill as air leader justified this appointment, although some might say, with reason, that Ernst Udet—who claimed to have shot down 60 enemy planes—should have been appointed.' In this wartime portrait, Udet wears the 'Blue Max' at the throat, as well as the Iron Cross and Imperial Flying Service Pilot's Badge at the right on his tunic.

Wilhelm Reinhard (1891–1918), who served as *Staffelführer* of *Jasta 6* from 26 November 1917 to 23 April 1918, and as commander of *JG 1* from 23 April 1918 until his death on 3 July 1918 in a fatal air accident. He had twenty aerial victories. Baron Manfred von Richthofen had stated in his 'military testament' of 10 March 1918, 'If I should not return, Lt Reinhard will assume command of the *Geschwader*.' In 1951, Butler and Young noted, 'On July 3, 1918, the two men [Goering and Reinhard] took off in succession from the Adlershorst [*sic*] aerodrome, near Berlin, to test a new Fokker fighter. Goering took the aircraft up first, banked, looped, and landed safely. He clambered out, and Reinhard replaced him in the cockpit. The Fokker climbed sweetly to 3,000 feet, and then the watchers on the ground saw the wings disintegrate. Its wing struts snapped, and the aircraft plummeted crazily to earth. Five days later, 1Lt Goering was posted to the *Richthofen Geschwader* in command. He had achieved a great ambition.' The source for this photo is *Cross & Cockade Journal* (Autumn 1982 issue), but I am somewhat doubtful that this actually is Reinhard, based on the only other shot allegedly of him that I have seen.

Reserve Lt Walter Hohndorf (1892–1917), 'Blue Max' recipient, who ended his career with twelve victories, at the wheel of this German Army staff car. Note the eagle logo on the door at bottom left of this frame.

A lineup of Fokker DR.I triplanes. *Aircraft: World Wars I and II* states, 'The Fokker DR.I triplane was built in response to the appearance of the Sopwith triplane ... It acquired a bad reputation after a series of crashes that were caused by faulty workmanship in the wing construction.'

Goering's caption to this photo of Fokker DR.I triplanes reads, 'Me in Colmar', 1917. After the Second World War, Col. Gen. Karl Koller—last Chief of the Luftwaffe General Staff—said of Goering in the Great War, 'He was not a good flier. He was not a good pilot. He was a good shot, [but] ... he was not very good as a pilot. He smashed several aircraft.'

A trio of triplanes lined up. Asked by US Navy Capt./Judge Michael A. Musmanno after the Second World War of Goering, 'Was he a courageous man?' Koller answered, 'Yes, he was a very good shot.'

Goering's caption is 'AEG plane at the landing at Colmar north', 1917. He stands at right in profile, with an Austrian Army officer at center.

'Jagdstaffel [Fighter Squadron] 26', 1917, with Goering (center), in flying suit, cap, and goggles. Imrie notes of this shot, '1st Lt Goering—*Staffelführer* of Squadron 27—briefing his pilots on Iseghem aerodrome, May 1918.' They stand in front of a Fokker DR.I triplane, with a Fokker D.VII at left.

'My machine [a Fokker DR.I triplane] at Stenay', June 1916. For armament, the triplane had two 7.92-mm Spandau machine guns, and a power plant of one 110-hp Oberursel UR.11 rotary engine. Its maximum speed was 102.5 mph at 13,123 feet, and its service ceiling was 20,013 feet. Entering service in 1917, its endurance was 1½ hours, and its weight at takeoff was 1,290 pounds. Its dimensions included a wingspan of 23 feet 7.88 inches, a length of 18 feet 11.16 inches, and a wing area of 200.9 square feet.

Imrie says of this photo, 'Fokker DR.I triplanes of *Jagdstaffel 27*. The pilot of the nearest aircraft is Lt Klimke, who survived the war with a total of 16 confirmed victories, May 1918.' Note, too, the rather amateurish-looking Maltese cross painted on the fuselage side.

The German Army ground crew assisted in the takeoff of this Fokker DR.I triplane.

'At Montmedy airfield', 1916, is Goering's caption to these takeoff and flight scenes of his Fokker DR.I triplane.

On 2 June 1918, Goering was awarded the *Pour le Mérite* by Kaiser Wilhelm II (fourth from left, with cane), Germany's last emperor. Here, Goering stands smiling (second from right). As the war ended, Goering shouted to his aide Karl Bodenschatz, 'The Frogs [French] want our Fokker D.VIIs. They've always wanted to get their hands on them, but they're not going to get them! Get the telephone rigged up, and tell them that, Bodenschatz!' (*US National Archives, College Park, MD*)

The Kaiser celebrated the thirtieth anniversary of his reign at Imperial General Headquarters on 15 June 1918, as seen here. *From left to right:* Field Marshal Paul von Hindenburg, unknown aide, Army Quartermaster General Erich Ludendorff (hand on right hip), unknown officer, the Kaiser (hand on left hip), unidentified aide, and Crown Prince Wilhelm (leaning against door jamb.) Barely six months later, only von Hindenburg retained his post. The Kaiser fired Ludendorff, and both he and his son fled to exile in Holland.

A pensive but angry-looking Goering stands next to his Fokker D.VII fighter plane for this later Sanke postcard portrait as *JG 1* commander in 1918. Note the brace of Spandau machine guns above him.

Rear view of a wing-damaged Fokker D.VII aircraft. One source states, 'Some 700 D.VIIs were in service at the time of the Armistice [11 November 1918], and the type was the only airplane specifically mentioned in the Treaty of Versailles for surrender to the Allies. After the First World War, Anthony Fokker returned to the Netherlands and resumed limited production of the D.VII.'

A trio of Fokker D.VIIs lined up. Another source comments, 'In the autumn of 1917, the German authorities invited manufacturers to submit single-seater fighter prototypes in the hopes of finding an aircraft that could regain ascendancy over the Allied fighters on the Western Front. In the trials the following January, the Fokker D.VII was unanimously acclaimed the best plane, and was put into mass production.'

Kilduff says of this rather well-known photo, 'A Fokker D.VII, possibly 324/18, that Goering flew when he commanded *Jagdgeschwader 1* in the summer of 1918.' Note that Goering (center, walking) still uses his cane in 1918, four years after the onset of his rheumatism. Of Goering's last aerial victory, Mosley adds, 'He didn't need to shoot down any more. He had made his point. It was teamwork that would motivate his Flying Circus from now on.'

'At the start', Goering captions this view of his Fokker D.VII fighter at left, as he suits up for another flight, aided by his ground crew. When the Great War ended, picture postcards of him had been sold all over Germany, thus making Goering a national hero at a time when the names of Hitler, Hess, Himmler, and Goebbels were years from being known at all.

Wearing a soft cap, Goering sits in the cockpit of his Fokker D.VII biplane fighter in 1918, as the lost war wound down. The aircraft was a single-seat fighter with one 185-hp BMW inline piston engine, had a maximum speed of 117 mph, could climb to 16,405 feet in 16 minutes, and carried a maximum take-off weight of 2,112 pounds. It had a wingspan of 29 feet 3.5 inches, a length of 22 feet 11.5 inches, a height of 9 feet 2.25 inches, a wing area of 221.4 square feet, and an armament of two fixed 7.92-mm machine guns.

Variations on a theme: photographs of captured Allied aircraft during the Great War. Kilduff has written of the first one, 'Goering took this photograph of Nieuport 17bis N. 3192, which he brought down on April 29, 1917.'

Goering appeared with the plane in the second one, of which he noted 'F-1/374'.

Goering's caption reads, 'British Sopwith Camel F-1'. In fact it was a Sopwith Scout of 66 Squadron which had arrived in France in March 1917. Squadron markings were changed in August 1917, so this photograph dates sometime between these months.

A pair of junked British RE.8 aircraft. The RE.8 was a two-seater reconnaissance aircraft of 1916, with a 150-hp RAF 4a engine, a wingspan of 42 feet 7 inches, a ceiling of 13,000 feet, and endurance of 4½ hours. Its armament consisted of the pilot's fixed Vickers machine gun, as well as one-two, flexible Lewis machine guns on the observer's Scarff mounting, and could carry a bomb load of 260 pounds.

I believe that this is either a modified French Nieuport or possibly a German aircraft captured first by the Allies, given Allied markings—as seen here—and recaptured by the Germans, and photographed in that altered state.

The British Sopwith Camel, first brought into service in the middle of 1917. Although it had some idiosyncrasies, once they had been mastered, it was found to be the ideal fighting plane. According to one account, 'It was the first British plane to have twin Vickers guns.' Goering shot one of these down in May 1918.

Crashed Allied aircraft.

Goering's caption is 'Captured French ... plane', 1914.

Possibly the interior of the 1914 French plane seen in the previous shot.

Above: 'The Nieuport shot down by Lt [Friedrich] Weitz at our Habsheim airfield' is Goering's caption to this 1917 shot. The Nieuport 17 was a 1916 single-seat scout aircraft, called by one source, 'The most popular fighter of the war … the favorite of such top aces as Ball, Bishop, Guynemer, and Nungesser.' Powered by a 110-hp Le Rhône rotary engine, it had a wingspan of 27 feet, a length of 19 feet 6 inches, a weight of 1,233 pounds when fully loaded, a speed of 107 mph at 6,500 feet, a ceiling of 17,400 feet, and an endurance of 2 hours. Its armament consisted of a single Lewis machine gun mounted on the upper wing that fired over the propeller, or 'a single fixed synchronized Vickers machine gun mounted on the fuselage forward of the pilot'.

Below: Goering's caption is 'English RE Eindecker', 1917.

Above: 'After an emergency landing, a modern French Spad fighter seen at Mühlhausen', Goering states of this 1917 shot. *Aircraft World Wars I and II* states, 'Spad produced some of the best combat aircraft of World War I. The Spad VII was a strong, stable gun platform with excellent turn of speed and good climb to 12,000 feet. It saw widespread service with every Allied air service. Some 6,000 were probably built.'

Below: A rear view of the same captured French Spad at Mülhausen in 1917. Of Goering as *JG 1* commander, Mosley recalls, 'He was determined that there would be only one prima donna in his outfit, and that would be himself. He would make the decisions, he would decide the tactics to be followed, and he would throw the tantrums if anything went wrong.' The Spad's armament consisted of a single fixed 8-mm Vickers machine gun forward, and it entered service in 1916. It was powered by a 150-hp Hispano-Suiza engine that provided a maximum speed of 119 mph at 6,500 feet. Its service ceiling was 17,500 feet, and it had an endurance of 2¼ hours. Its weight was 1,632 pounds, and it had a wingspan of 25 feet, 8 inches. It was 20 feet, 3.5 inches long and 7 feet high.

Goering's caption reads, 'Me in a [British] Sopwith', 1917. This is probably the Sopwith Scout A6194 pictured earlier. The Scout was commonly known as the Sopwith Pup. This nickname arose because pilots considered it to be the 'pup' of the larger two-seat Sopwith 1½ Strutter.

Goering (center) captioned these photos 'Metz', 1916. He is smiling and wearing an open fur-collared overcoat, with 1914 Iron Cross ribbon, Iron Cross, and Observer's Badge visible on his tunic.

'At the airfield', 1917. Goering is seated at the left and Lörzer at the right. The man in the center is unknown.

'After the lineup of Jagdstaffel 26 at Colmar', 1917.

Goering sits at the far right of the table, with others unknown, pre-'Blue Max'.

Bronnenkant captions this photo thus: '... Most of the *Pour le Mérite* airmen who attended the October-November 1918 Adlershof fighter trials ... *Left to right:* Lt Josef Veltjens, 1st Lt Oskar von Boenigk, Capt. Eduard *Ritter* von Schleich, Capt. Bruno Lörzer, 1st Lt Hermann Goering, 1st Lt Ernst Udet, Lt Heinrich Bongartz, Lt Josef Jacobs, and Lt Paul Baumer.'

Goering's caption reads, 'Fighter Squadron 26 at Habsheim airfield', 1917. Kilduff has added: 'Early members of *Jagdstaffel 26* posed for this photo in late February 1917. They are, seated *(left to right): Offizierstellvertreter* [Acting Officer] Fritz Lörzer, younger brother of Bruno Lörzer; and Lt Karl Wewer. Standing *(left to right):* Acting Officer Rudolf Weckbrodt, Sgt. Langer, PFC Hansen, 1st Lt Bruno Lörzer, two unknown, Lt Hermann Goering, Sgt. Richard Linke, Reserve Lt Walter Blume, Reserve Lt Hans Auer, and Reserve Lt Theodor Rumpel.'

Above: Of this photo, Kilduff states, 'In late October 1918—less than two weeks before the end of World War I—leading German fighter pilots attended one last party hosted by the Pfalz Aeroplane Works at the Adlon Hotel on Unter den Linden (Under the linden trees) in downtown Berlin.' Bronnenkant noted earlier, 'Lt Josef Veltjens and other airmen attending a dinner hosted by Alfred Eversbusch (Pfalz Company) during the ... Adlershof fighter trials. Eversbusch sits at far right, and next to him are: Capt. Bruno Lörzer, 1st Lt Ernst Udet, Capt. Eduard *Ritter* von Schleich, 1st Lt Oskar von Boenigk, Lt Josef Jacobs, unknown, Lt Franz Ray, and other unknowns. Across the table—starting at the right, are 1st Lt. Hermann Goering [eyes shut], Lt Friedrich Mallinckrodt, Lt Heinrich Bongartz, Lt Hans Klein, 1st Lt Fritz von Falkenhayn, Lt Veltjens, unknown, Lt Paul Baumer, Lt Hans-Joachim Rolfes, Lt Walter Dingel, and unknown.' Of this banquet, Kilduff concludes, 'The most famous contemporary dancer, Miss Lucy Kieselhausen [danced] totally in the nude.'

Below: At the October-November 1918 fighter aircraft trials at Adlershof outside Berlin, *left to right:* Bruno Lörzer, Goering, Lothar von Richthofen, and others unknown.

APPENDIX 1

Imperial German Crown Prince Wilhelm (1882–1951) Goering's First Patron

Aside from his passions for women, cars, and hunting, Imperial German Crown Prince Wilhelm correctly predicted—in 1914—that Germany had already lost the First World War.

The First Battle of the Marne had just been won by the French Army when—in the first half of November 1914—American Hearst Corporation journalist Karl von Wiegand paid a visit to the commander of the German 5th Army at Stenay in occupied France. He was stunned to hear its chief—Imperial Crown Prince Wilhelm of the reigning House of Hohenzollern—assert in a private aside, 'We have lost the war. It will go on for a long time, but lost it is already.'

He was right, showing a clear-headedness that few of his contemporaries—including His Imperial Majesty Kaiser Wilhelm II, whose eldest son and heir to the throne he was—gave him enough credit for. His grandfather held similar posts in the wars of 1866–71.

As Hermann Goering's Army commander in the field, he also played a major role in the young airman's career by taking an interest in him as early as during the first year of the Great War. In this way, His Imperial Highness became Goering's first great patron in life. Had Wilhelm become Kaiser himself, most likely Goering would have risen fast in his service, just as he later did under his second great patron, Nazi Führer Adolf Hitler.

Had Wilhelm acceded to the throne in 1918 upon the abdication of his father, he might have reigned until his death in 1951, for 33 years—therefore, a rule three years longer than His Majesty's. It was not to be, however, for when his father abdicated, he did likewise, and thus came to an end the Imperial and Royal House of Hohenzollern as the rulers of Prussia and Germany.

Following is a selection of photos of the Crown Prince from Goering's own albums during the Great War.

Imperial German Crown Prince Wilhelm (1882–1951) in a formal portrait at the age of 50 in 1932, in a photograph that he often sent to friends.

Above and below: The Crown Prince (right, in light uniform jacket) and his staff at headquarters during the First World War. To his immediate right is his Chief of Staff, German Army Lt-Gen. Schmidt von Knobelsdorf. Upon conferring the 5th Army command on his son, his father the Kaiser told him, 'Whatever he advises you, you must do.' The other officers present at left are unknown. For the second photo caption, Goering has written, 'The Crown Prince with his general staff during the Battle of Longwy'. Photos taken by Goering, 1914.

The Imperial German Crown Prince at center, as seen in the field in France with his staff at Stenay, 1914. In the first photo, he holds a bouquet of flowers from a well-wisher; in the second, he looks directly into the lens of Goering's camera; in the third, he turns his head to talk with an aide. The Crown Prince was not well thought of by the average German soldier, however, and was seen as a thoughtless playboy who occasionally tossed them cigarettes, his whippets in tow.

His Imperial Highness Crown Prince Wilhelm (second from left, wearing Uhlan helmet and balancing a curved cavalry saber) was the man Allied cartoonists loved to caricature as 'Little Willy', in contrast to his bellicose father. Here, the commander of the assembled guard at right greets him, just before the troop review. Note also the sentry at left, presenting arms.

Goering's own photos of the Crown Prince (left, center) and visiting King Ludwig III of Bavaria 'trooping the line' of assembled soldiers in honor of His Majesty's visit to German 5th Army headquarters at Stenay in occupied France, 1915. Goering's own one-word photo caption is simply 'Kavalcade' (Parade).

Fifth and sixth from left, the Crown Prince and his guest the King of Bavaria review the parading troops passing by at right, 1915. Note the informal swagger stick baton in His Majesty's right hand, held at a downward angle.

King Ludwig III of Bavaria (third from right) about to decorate Lt Hermann Goering (at far right) standing at attention, 1915.

Another view of the same decorations ceremony in the field, 1915. The King wears the white ceremonial belt (back to camera) eighth from the left moving right, while the Crown Prince stands seven more figures to the right, wearing Uhlan helmet, back to camera, and with his left hand resting on the pommel of his cavalry saber.

A final view of the same event, this time from the front, with the Crown Prince at center wearing Uhlan helmet, and the King at right, wearing white ceremonial belt and white beard.

Kilduff has captioned this photo, 'Recognizing a good opportunity, Goering photographed Crown Prince Wilhelm [back to the camera, clasping his hands] before the maiden flight of the new AEG G.III G 54/15 on April 30, 1916.' I believe that he is mistaken, and that Goering is the figure standing to the left of His Imperial Highness, facing toward the camera.

'Goering also photographed the crash of AEG G.III G 54/15 after it had landed on soft soil that could not support the airplane's weight,' is Kilduff's caption.

Goering's own field portrait of Crown Prince Wilhelm of Germany.

Above left: Goering's caption is 'The Crown Prince with us and his staff'. Crown Prince Wilhelm stands near the open car door second from right and puffing on a cigarette. Goering is smiling and wearing goggles on his cap at Wilhelm's immediate right; fifth from left is Bruno Lörzer, also smiling. The other officers are unidentified.

Above right: Goering's photo of Crown Prince Wilhelm teeing off near 5th Army Headquarters at Stenay in occupied France, 1915.

On 6 March 1939—during the Nazi Third Reich—Goering emulates his former Imperial master in the sport of golf, at San Remo in Italy. Goering was the only top Nazi leader to play golf.

Above left: Former Imperial German Crown Prince Wilhelm strides forth, wearing Death's Head Hussar's busby, overcoat, and uniform in the 1930s, after his return from his Dutch exile.

Above right: Former Imperial German Crown Prince Wilhelm (right) talks with Reichstag President Hermann Goering (left) on the steps of that building in Berlin in 1933, after the Nazi Party had been appointed to office by President von Hindenburg. Goering wears Nazi Party brown uniform, while Wilhelm wears the undress uniform of the famed Death's Head Hussars. Both he and Goering also have their 'Blue Max' medals at the throat.

APPENDIX 2

Curtain of Death: The Synchronized Machine Gun

At first, there was no armament of any kind in the airplanes of the First World War, but soon pistols—and then rifles—found their way aloft, and there were several early attempts to mount machine guns as well on both sides.

Lee Kennett in his 1991 study *The First Air War, 1914–1918* writes:

> South of Dixude, [French] aviator Roland Garros brought down an Aviatik with shots from a machine gun. [This brief notice in the French Army's morning communiqué for 2 April 1915, picked up and amplified by the Paris press, had considerable repercussions on French aeronautical circles, and among the public as well.]
>
> Roland Garros was a well-known aviator before the war, and the first to fly across the Mediterranean in 1913. Now—having mounted a machine gun on his Morane—Garros was one of the pioneers in the art of aerial combat. His name came to public attention again as he shot down a second and a third German plane, and then was himself forced down and taken prisoner—all in the month of April 1915.
>
> Roland Garros was one of an initial group of aerial 'heroes' produced in the first months of war. Most of them, like Garros, had names already familiar to the public because of their prewar exploits.

In *Aces High: The War in the Air over the Western Front, 1914–18*, Alan Clark adds:

> Lt Roland Garros—who had been a famous stunt pilot before the war in Morane-Saulnier monoplanes—visited Raymond Saulnier in December 1914, and arranged to have his own airplane fitted out with the new device for a forward-firing machine gun. The interrupter gear was not fitted, Garros relying on the deflection plates only to ward off the bullets that would otherwise have struck his airscrew.
>
> The work proceeded at a leisurely pace, and it was not until the end of March that Garros took to the air, but his success was immediate, and electrifying. In just over a fortnight [fourteen days] he had shot down five German airplanes—an unprecedented score for that period [and also making him the first ace of the Great War].

> But on April 19th, he was brought down by ground fire while strafing a column of enemy infantry on the road near Courtrai. Garros' attempts to set fire to his airplane were unsuccessful, and the Germans immediately set about copying and modifying it.

Mosley, writing in 1974, describes the effect that Garros had on the German side:

> One day in April 1915, the whole nature of the air war changed. Four Albatros observer planes from a 5th Army base were cruising over French territory, on their way back from a reconnaissance mission. They were unarmed, but since they were flying at 10,000 feet, they felt completely safe from any kind of attack; even those French planes whose observers had now begun to emulate Goering and take a machine gun aboard could not possibly reach this height with such a load in the cockpit.
>
> When one of the Albatros pilots sighted a French monoplane coming toward them and signaled the fact to his comrades, no one broke formation, and none of them felt any particular concern. What could one unarmed French monoplane do to them?
>
> What they could not guess was that not only was the plane armed, but that it was flown by a remarkable Frenchman named Roland Garros who was about to make two of the German planes the first victims of a new form of aerial combat. For the first time in aerial warfare, he was trying out a light machine gun that fired bullets between the blades of his propeller.
>
> The weapon was not completely synchronized, and in the course of firing, Roland Garros knew that some of the bullets would tear great lumps out of his props, even though he had reinforced them with bands of steel, but what did that matter if he could shoot down a Hun?
>
> He came straight at the enemy quartet and opened fire at close range, and the plane on the near side wing crumpled, caught fire, and fell away at once. As the other three scattered in terrified confusion, he rounded on them, and shot down another before the remaining two disappeared into the clouds, and his own machine began to yaw wildly.
>
> He had shot one of his props almost completely away, but that did not faze him, for he had expected it—and cutting out the engine he turned, and began gliding earthward, back toward his station, and a safe place to land. Next day—with his new propeller fitted—he was up again and on the hunt.
>
> In four combats in the next 18 days, Garros shot down five German planes, but he did more than that. He spread first disbelief and then panic among German air strategists. How could this happen? How could a monoplane carry a machine gun that seemed to shoot right through its own propellers?
>
> On April 19th, 18 days after the first encounter, they found out. On that day, Garros was on his way toward a new kill when engine trouble stalled his plane, and he had to glide down for a forced landing on German territory, where he was taken prisoner before he could set fire to his plane. Garros was taken off to an interrogation centre, and his plane hauled away for minute examination.
>
> It so happened that one of the men who was designing planes for the German Air Force was a young Dutchman named Anthony Hermann Gerard Fokker, and because the new plane which he had just produced was a monoplane of a type similar to that flown by

Garros, he was called in to examine the captured machine and its alarming new weapon. Could he design something like it?

Fokker—who would soon be recognized as one of the world's greatest aircraft designers—knew nothing about guns, but after a cursory examination of the weapon in the captured plane, he told the anxious Germans that he could do much better.

This was practically a suicide weapon, he told the Germans. He pointed to the steel-reinforced propellers. 'A bullet hitting this as it passed through could tear off a chip big enough to smash the engine or kill the pilot as it flew back at him. Such a gun can only be used when it is really synchronized.' But that wasn't possible, said the Germans.

It was possible, replied Anthony Fokker calmly. He remembered his boyhood days in Holland when he and his companions had spent their time trying to throw stones between the flailing arms of the windmills in the fields around Haarlem. There was a trick to it. You waited until the sail was vertical, and then you threw straight at it, and by the time the stone reached it, there was a space for it to pass through.

Somewhere, somehow, there was a lesson in that which could be adapted to a bullet rather than a windmill sail. Fokker—a supremely confident man—had promised his sceptical German masters that he would solve the problem and produce a perfected version of the Garros gun within a week.

The remarkable thing is that he brought the project in ahead of time, working with three trusted assistants for 48 hours straight, he found the secret of synchronization, and six days later had towed a monoplane equipped with a machine gun to Berlin for a demonstration.

It was not much later that Fokker learned that a similar solution to the problem had already been patented in 1912 by Franz Schneider, but had been filed away by the Germans and forgotten. The Germans looked at the device and expressed disbelief that it would work. Fokker gave them a demonstration on the ground. They were still sceptical about its chances in the air, so Fokker took the plane up to 900 feet, directed the nose at a pile of old debris in a corner of the field, and opened fire.

The bullets not only slashed the pile to pieces, but also ricocheted all over the field, forcing the German experts to run for their lives. Fokker had done it deliberately. 'When they took to their heels,' Fokker wrote later, 'I decided that they would never forget that the gun shot from the air as well as from the ground.'

Still, the Germans demanded final proof that the new weapon would work, and that could only be achieved in actual combat in the air, with the gun actually shooting down an enemy plane. If Fokker wanted the money he had been promised for his weapon, it was up to him to show it would work, and they shrugged their shoulders when he pointed out that he was Dutch, neutral, and a civilian.

The upshot was that in mid-May 1915, Anthony Fokker found himself dressed in the uniform of a German lieutenant, a false identity card in his pocket, taking a buffet lunch and hock with Crown Prince Wilhelm and a round table of German pilots at a chateau close to the airfield at Douai.

Among his lunchtime companions was Hermann Goering and Bruno Lörzer, both of them excited at the potential of the weapon that Fokker was due to demonstrate over the front that afternoon.

Goering was eager to see the performance of the new weapon, which he recognized as a crucial development in air warfare, but it was no use asking permission to go along. The Albatros in which he and Lörzer flew was too slow for Fokker's monoplane. When he became friends with Fokker in later years, Goering afterward reminded him of that luncheon party and remembered that he had patted him on the back, 'Because you looked so miserable, and hardly touched your food.'

'I was miserable,' Fokker replied. 'I kept wondering how I had got into such a fix! I was a non-combatant, and I was going up to make a kill. If I were shot down or landed on enemy territory, I would be executed as a spy—and rightly.'

The flight that afternoon was something of an anti-climax, because no enemy planes were sighted, but on the eighth day, Fokker was flying over Douai at 6,000 feet when he saw a French Farman two-seater. He dived toward him, but the Frenchman—utterly ignorant of the weapon that was now being sighted on him—took no action to get out of the way.

'As the distance narrowed between us,' Fokker wrote later, 'the plane grew larger in my sights. My imagination could picture my shots puncturing the gasoline tanks ... Even if my bullets failed to kill the pilot and observer, the ship would fall down in flames. I had my finger on the trigger ... I had no personal enmity towards the French. I was merely trying to prove that a certain mechanism I had invented would work.

'By this time, I was near enough to open fire, and the French airmen were watching me curiously, wondering no doubt why I was flying up behind them. In another instant, it would be all over for them. Suddenly, I decided that the whole job could go to hell! It was too much like 'cold meat' to suit me. I had no stomach for the whole business, nor any wish to kill Frenchmen for Germans. Let them go do their own killing!'

The Germans were astonished and infuriated, and threats and insults were used to persuade him to change his mind, but Fokker was adamant. Finally, it was agreed that he would instruct a German fighter pilot in the use of the gun, and a man who was to become one of Germany's greatest aces—Lt Oswald Boelcke—was picked for the task.

He shot down his unsuspecting victim on his third flight, and the German air strategists were convinced at last of the vital importance of the new weapon. Orders were given to fit it into all fighter planes.

Lt Max Immelmann—who was to give his name to a classic manoeuvre in air combat—was the second pilot to be given a fixed-gun Fokker monoplane. 'It was an improved model, designated the Fokker E-2, with a 100 hp Oberursel engine in place of the 80 hp Argus,' wrote Aaron Norman. 'Within three or four weeks, half a dozen E-2s were in service at the front.

'Immelmann, Boelcke, and the other Fokker pilots—who numbered 16 by the middle of June—had only to spot an enemy plane and get above it or behind it to guarantee a kill. They found that by slightly wobbling the monoplane's nose in circular fashion, they could emit—instead of a straight stream of bullets—a cone of fire, trapping their victim in the centre, who, no matter which way he turned to escape, met a curtain of death.'

By the summer of 1915, the German Air Force was master of the skies over the Western Front, but not for long.

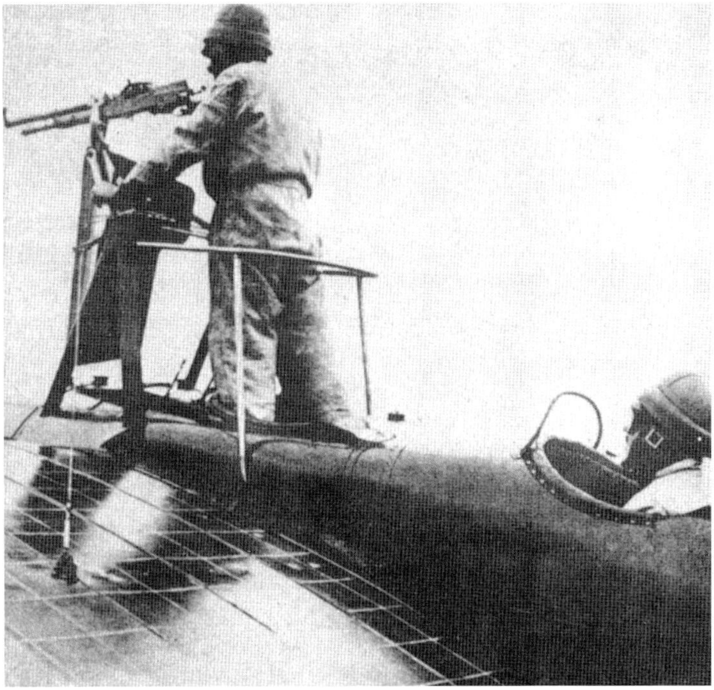

A British aircraft with a machine gun mounted in 1912, before the outbreak of the war.

An early attempt at mounting a machine gun on a French aircraft in February 1914, before the start of the Great War that August.

The man who started all the commotion in April 1915, Lt Roland Garros with a pre-war Morane-Saulnier monoplane. He escaped from German captivity and was later killed in action. He made aviation history by being the first to fly the Mediterranean Sea in peacetime, and in wartime with his aerial machine gun.

Lt Garros (left) prepares to go on patrol in his Morane aircraft in April 1915. In eighteen days he shot down five German aircraft.

Goering's own album view of famed Dutch aircraft designer Anthony Fokker (1890–1939) with one of his famous Fokker D.1 triplanes in German-occupied France. His synchronization of machine gun with propeller blades revolutionized air warfare in the First World War in 1915.

An instructional mock-up of the Fokker gun gear. The handle at lower right turned the cam that operated the interrupter gear through rods and levers. Henri Hegener in *Fokker: The Man and the Aircraft* wrote, 'The following Friday, he [Fokker] returned to Air Service Headquarters with an actual synchronized machine gun as used in subsequent aerial warfare. The invention and development had all been completed in 48 hours of day-and-night work, after the essential method had been conceived. Fokker had connected the firing mechanism of the weapon—by means of cams and levers—to the engine in such a way that it could shoot only if the propeller blade was clear of the barrel of the gun. Having tested the gear in an M.5K monoplane—firing across Lake Schwerin—he hitched the monoplane by the tail to his Peugeot touring car, and set off for Berlin.'

The rods and levers operated by the cam on the engine crankshaft are clearly shown on this Albatros C.I, 1915. Hegener in *Fokker: The Man and the Aircraft* wrote, 'Garros had fitted bullet-deflecting plates to his propeller, and the Germans were not slow to copy this device, but their results were disappointing. Whereas the French bullets with a copper coating were effectively deflected, the German bullets—with a chrome plating—shot the blades to pieces ... Fokker was sent for at Schwerin ... So Fokker came to Berlin, heard what was required of him, thought awhile, and promised that within a few days he would devise a firing system not only equal to, but better than, what the French had conceived.'

German ace Oswald Boelcke wearing the 'Blue Max' at the throat, as well as the Iron Cross below it and an actual Iron Cross at lower right on his tunic. Capt. Boelcke was one of the first pilots to test Fokker's new weapon in actual combat. Born on 19 May 1891, he received the 'Blue Max' on 12 January 1916—Goering's birthday—and also the very same day as Max Immelmann, but was ranked as the first fighter pilot to receive it. He died at age 25 as the result of a tragic mid-air collision on 28 October 1916.

Above: Goering's own photograph of the legendary ace Oswald Boelcke (third from left in the first row, right hand on hip), seen with fellow German aviators in the First World War. A detail of this photo was first published in 2008 in book form by Lance J. Bronnenkant PhD. This, however, is the full frame of that photo, as seen in Goering's albums. Dr Bronnenkant's earlier caption reads 'Hptm. [Capt.] Oswald Boelcke in the company of members of *Artillerie-Flieger-Abteilung* [Artillery Flight Section] 203, presumably at their base near Jametz. He had been invited over from Sivry by their CO [commanding officer] Hptm. Vogt [possibly third from the right, front row] to provide them with fighter protection during a reconnaissance mission that, according to Boelcke's correspondence home, occurred at some point between 12 and 18 June 1916. This shot was probably taken around then. Note that Oblt. [1Lt] Stefan Kirmaier [second from the right, front row], who had joined the unit on 10 June shortly before the mission, is not wearing his Pilot's Badge—something he would not earn until 11 July 1916.'

Below: Learning how to shoot from a moving vehicle, a British airman fires his machine gun from a simulated cockpit that moves along rails. The machine gun is a British Lewis gun with ammunition drum atop it. According to the Smithsonian Air & Space Museum, 'Gunnery training was even more cursory than flight instruction. Many pilots received only one day of instruction before leaving for the front. Although pilots were expected to sharpen their marksmanship during their first few missions, many were killed before they ever fired their guns in combat.'

Lt Hermann Goering (under the 't' at left) waits his turn at machine gun practice, firing with other German pilots during a lull in the air war.

A rear view of Goering's own mounted Spandau machine gun on the cowling of his fighter aircraft.